Beyond Learning

Interventions: Education, Philosophy & Culture
Michael A. Peters & Colin Lankshear, Series Editors

Education, Globalization, and the State in the Age of Terrorism
    edited by Michael A. Peters (2005)

Beyond Learning: Democratic Education for a Human Future
    by Gert J. J. Biesta (2006)

Democracy, Ethics, and Education: A Thin Communitarian
    Approach
    by Mark Olssen (2007)

Beyond Learning

Democratic Education
for a Human Future

Gert J. J. Biesta

Paradigm Publishers
Boulder • London

Copyright © 2006 by Paradigm Publishers

Published in the United States by Paradigm Publishers, 3360 Mitchell Lane, Suite E, Boulder, Colorado 80301 USA.

Paradigm Publishers is the trade name of Birkenkamp & Company, LLC, Dean Birkenkamp, President and Publisher.

Library of Congress Cataloging-in-Publication Data
Biesta, Gert.
  Beyond learning : democratic education for a human future / Gert J. J. Biesta.
    p. cm. — (Interventions)
  Includes bibliographical references and index.
  ISBN-13: 978-1-59451-233-9 (hardcover)
  ISBN-10: 1-59451-233-7 (hardcover)
    1. Education—Philosophy. 2. Education—Aims and objectives.
  3. Education, Humanistic.   I. Title. II. Series: Interventions
  (Paradigm Publishers)
  LB14.7.B529 2006
  370.11'5—dc22

                                                              2006001592

Printed and bound in the United States of America on acid-free paper that meets the standards of the American National Standard for Permanence of Paper for Printed Library Materials.

Designed and Typeset by Straight Creek Bookmakers.

10 09 08 07 06
5 4 3 2 1

Contents

Acknowledgments

This book is based upon ideas that were developed over the past decade in a range of articles, chapters, and presentations. I believe that, taken together, these ideas amount to a theory of education or, as I put it in the book, to a way to understand and approach education. I neither claim nor expect that the theory of education put forward in this book will be able to address all the issues educators are faced with. But I do believe that my reflections respond to one of the most urgent questions in the world of today: the question of how to live with others in a world of plurality and difference. In this book I challenge the idea that we can only live together in such a world if we can provide a common definition of our humanity. Instead I explore the implications for the ways in which we educate if we treat the question of what it means to be human as a radically open question: a question that can only be answered by engaging in education rather than a question that needs to be answered before we can educate.

One of the central ideas of the book is that we come into the world as unique individuals through the ways in which we respond responsibly to what and who is other. I argue that the responsibility of the educator not only lies in the cultivation of "worldly spaces" in which the encounter with otherness and difference is a real possibility, but that it extends to asking "difficult questions": questions that summon us to respond responsively and responsibly to otherness and difference in our own, unique ways.

Although this book deals with educational theories and philosophies, my aim has not been to write a book for theorists. My hope is that educators across a wide range of different settings will recognize the issues discussed in this book and, more importantly, will be able to formulate their own responses to the ideas presented in the chapters that follow.

I have developed my ideas in response to the work of several philosophers and theorists, most notably Hannah Arendt, Emmanuel Levinas, Michel Foucault, and Zygmunt Bauman. I have also been inspired by the writings of Jacques Derrida, Jacques Rancière, Jan Masschelein, and Bernhard Tschumi. I am indebted to all of them for their inspiration and provocation. The chapters in this book are also responses in a more direct sense, in that earlier versions of most chapters were written in response to invitations for conference and seminar presentations and contributions to journals and books. I am particularly grateful to Barbara Stengel, who triggered my thinking about learning, to Carl-Anders Säfström, who stimulated my reflections on identity and difference, to Alison Jones and Nick Burbules for their invitation to explore the difficult nature of education, to Jan Masschelein and Maarten Simons for the opportunity to investigate the architecture of education, and to Tomas Englund and Carsten Ljunggren for providing me with the space for developing my ideas about education and democracy. Lars Løvlie suggested, long ago, that I had "something to say." He gave me the confidence to start working on this book, while Deborah Osberg and Rob Lawy gave me the confidence to finish it. Colleagues and students in Sweden, Denmark, Norway, Switzerland, South Africa, the United States, Canada, and the UK provided me with helpful feedback on my ideas, and their responses also indicated that questions about the role of education in a democratic society, a society committed to plurality and difference, are central to the work of educators in many countries around the world. I wish to thank Michael Peters for the invitation to publish this book in his series. I also wish to thank Dean Birkenkamp for his confidence in the project and for his continuous support.

There are times in life when the question of knowing if one can think differently than one thinks, and perceive differently than one sees, is absolutely necessary if one is to go on looking and reflecting at all.

Michel Foucault (1985, 8)

To be human means to live as if one were not a being among beings.

Emmanuel Levinas (1985, 100)

Education is the point at which we decide whether we love the world enough to assume responsibility for it and by the same token to save it from that ruin which, except for renewal, except for the coming of the new and young, would be inevitable. And education, too, is where we decide whether we love our children enough not to expel them from our world and leave them to their own devices, nor to strike from their hands their changes of undertaking something new, something unforeseen by us.

Hannah Arendt (1977a, 196)

Prologue

Education and the Question of Being Human

To be human means to live as if one were not a being among beings.

—Emmanuel Levinas

What does it mean to be human? What is the definition of humanity? What is the measure of humanity? What does it mean to lead a human life? These are age-old questions with which philosophers have occupied themselves ever since they turned their gaze away from the natural world toward the world of human beings. To say that these are philosophical questions is not to say that they are merely theoretical questions. An answer to the question of what it means to be human can have far-reaching practical consequences as well, both in those cases in which there is a positive answer to this question (such as in the Universal Declaration of Human Rights) and in those cases in which a certain definition of what it means to be human is used to exclude some from the realm of human interaction.

1

The question as to what it means to be human is also, and perhaps even first of all, an *educational* question. Education, be it the education of children, the education of adults, or the education of other "newcomers," is after all always an intervention into someone's life—an intervention motivated by the idea that it will make this life somehow better: more complete, more rounded, more perfect—and maybe even more human. Many educational practices are configured as practices of socialization. They are concerned with the insertion of newcomers into an existing cultural and sociopolitical order. This is not unimportant, since it equips newcomers with the cultural tools needed for participation in a particular form of life and at the same time secures cultural and social continuity. But we cannot be too naive about this, because these processes also contribute to the reproduction of existing inequalities—unwillingly or, in those cases in which education is utilized to conserve particular practices and traditions, also willingly. (This is not to say that such strategies are necessarily nonprogressive. The U.S. educationalist George Counts also called himself a conservative because he believed in the conservation of radical ideas.) Education is, however, not exclusively the servant of the existing order. There is an important countercurrent in educational thought and practice in which education is seen as the servant of the individual. Here the task and purpose of education is *not* understood in terms of discipline, socialization, or moral training, that is, in terms of insertion and adaptation, but is focused on the cultivation of the human person or, to put it differently, on the cultivation of the individual's *humanity* (see Løvlie et al., 2003).

By far the oldest way of thinking along these lines can be found in the tradition of *Bildung*.[1] *Bildung* stands for an educational ideal that emerged in Greek society and that, through its adoption in Roman culture, humanism, neohumanism, and the Enlightenment, became one of the central notions of the modern Western educational tradition (see Klafki 1986). Central to this tradition is the question of what constitutes an educated or cultivated human being. Initially the answer to this question was given in terms of the *contents* of *Bildung*. An educated person was the one who had acquired a clearly defined set of knowledge and values; it was the one who was properly socialized into a particular tradition. An important step was taken when the activity of the acquisition of the contents of *Bildung* became itself recognized as a constitutive aspect of the process of *Bildung* (e.g., by Johann Gotfried von Herder, Johann Heinrich Pestalozzi, and Wilhelm Von Humbolt). Since then *Bildung* has always been understood as self-*Bildung* (see Gadamer 2001).

The foundations of *modern* educational theory and practice were laid when the tradition of *Bildung* became intertwined with the Enlightenment. Emmanuel Kant provided the classical definition of enlightenment as "man's [sic] release from his self-incurred tutelage" and defined tutelage (or, in other translations: immaturity) as "man's [sic] inability to make use of his understanding without direction from another" (Kant 1992 [1784], 90). This immaturity is self-incurred, Kant wrote, "when its cause lies not in lack of reason but in lack of resolution and courage to use it without direction from another. *Sapere aude!* 'Have courage to use your own understanding!'—that is the motto of Enlightenment" (Kant 1992 [1784], 90).

The most important aspect of Kant's call for rational autonomy—for autonomy based upon reason—was that he did not conceive of this capacity as a contingent historical possibility, but saw it instead as something that was an inherent part of human nature. Kant described the "propensity and vocation to free thinking" as man's "ultimate destination" and the "aim of his existence" (Kant 1982, 701). To block progress in enlightenment would therefore be "a crime against human nature" (Kant 1992 [1784], 93). Interestingly enough—and this is particularly significant for the destiny of modern education since the Enlightenment—Kant also argued that the propensity for free thinking could *only* be brought about through education. He not only wrote that man "is the only creature that has to be educated" (Kant 1982, 697), but also argued that "man can only become man"—that is, a rational autonomous being—"through education" (Kant 1982, 699).

With Kant the rationale for the educational process became founded "on the humanist idea of a certain kind of subject who has the inherent potential to become self-motivated and self-directing," while the task of education became one of bringing out or releasing this potential "so that subjects become fully autonomous and capable of exercising their individual and intentional agency" (Usher and Edwards 1994, 24–25). Modern education thus became based on a particular *truth* about the nature and destiny of the human being, while the connection between rationality, autonomy, and education became the "Holy Trinity" of the Enlightenment project. This was not only the case in approaches that more or less directly followed on from the Kantian framework, such as the educational theories of Piaget and Kohlberg. The idea(l) of rational autonomy also became the cornerstone of critical approaches to education that took their inspiration from Hegel, Marx, and neo-Marxism—such as the work of Paulo Freire and North American and Continental versions of critical pedagogy (see Biesta 1998a). Along both lines education became understood as the process that helps people to develop their rational potential so that they can become autonomous, self-directing individualist, while rationality became the modern marker of what it means to be human (which left all those who were considered to be not or not-yet rational, including children, in a difficult position).

In this book I explore what might follow if we try to overcome the humanist foundations of modern education. I explore, in other words, how we might understand and "do" education if we no longer assume that we can know the essence and nature of the human being—or, to put it differently, if we treat the question of what it means to be human as a radically *open* question, a question that can only be answered by engaging in education rather than as a question that needs to be answered *before* we can engage in education. For the purpose of this book I understand "humanism" in the philosophical sense. It stands for the assumption that it is possible to know and articulate the essence or nature of the human being and to use this knowledge as a foundation for our educational and political efforts. Humanism, as Emmanuel Levinas has put it, thus entails "the recognition of an invariable essence named 'Man,' the affirmation of his central place in the economy of the Real and of his value which [engenders] all values" (Levinas 1990, 277).

But why should we try to overcome humanism? Why should we try to leave it behind? There can be no doubt that humanism has been an important and in some cases successful strategy for safeguarding the humanity of the human being. Yet the question is whether it can still be an effective strategy today. In this book I take a lead from philosophers who have raised fundamental questions about both the *possibility* and the *desirability* of the "strategy" of humanism. One of these philosophers is Emmanuel Levinas. For Levinas the "crisis of humanism in our society" began with the "inhuman events of recent history" (Levinas 1990, 279). For Levinas these not only include the inhumanities of "[t]he 1914 War, the Russian Revolution refuting itself in Stalinism, fascism, Hitlerism, the 1939–45 War, atomic bombings, genocide and uninterrupted war," but are also entailed in "a science that calculates the real without always thinking it," a "liberal politics and administration that suppresses neither exploitation nor war," and "a socialism that gets entangled in bureaucracy" (Levinas 1990, 279). For Levinas the crisis of humanism is, however, not located in these inhumanities as such, but first of all in humanism's inability to effectively counter such inhumanities, and secondly, and more importantly, in the fact that many of these inhumanities were actually based on and motivated by a particular definition of what it means to be human. He therefore concludes that "[h]umanism has to be denounced ... because it is not *sufficiently* human" (Levinas 1981, 128; emphasis added).

This way of putting the problem of humanism is reminiscent of Martin Heidegger, who in his work has also exposed the shortcomings of humanism in Western culture. In his *Letter on Humanism*, originally published in 1947, Heidegger wrote that humanism had to be opposed "because it does not set the *humanitas* of man [*sic*] high enough" (Heidegger 1993 [1947], 233–234). For Heidegger one of the key problems with humanism is that it is *metaphysical* (see Heidegger 1993 [1947], 226). By this he means that humanism's answer to the question of what it means to be human focuses on the essence or nature of the human being, on the human being as a thing, and not, as Heidegger thinks we should do, on the *Being* of this being, that is, on the *existence* of the human being, on the ways in which the human being exists in the world (see Heidegger 1993 [1947], 228). According to Heidegger humanism not only doesn't ask the question of the *Being* of the human being—and thus can only apprehend the human being as a thing among other things. Because of its metaphysical approach "humanism even impedes the question by neither recognizing nor understanding it" (Heidegger 1993 [1947], 228).[2]

The problem with humanism, therefore, is that it posits a *norm of humaneness,* a norm of what it means to be human, and in doing so excludes those who do not live up to or are unable to live up to this norm (see Honig 1993). At the dawn of the twenty-first century we know all too well that this is not just a theoretical possibility. Many of the atrocities that have become the markers of the twentieth century—such as the holocaust and the genocides in Cambodia, Rwanda, and Bosnia—were actually based on a definition of what counts as, and more importantly *who* counts as human. From an educational point of view the problem with humanism is that it specifies a norm of what it means to be human *before* the actual manifestation of "instances" of humanity. Humanism specifies what the child, student, or "newcomer" must become before giving them the opportunity to show who they are and who they want to be. Humanism thus seems unable to be open to the possibility that newcomers might radically alter our understanding of what it means to be human. Humanism seems to foreclose the possibility that the newborn child might be a new Ghandi, that the student in our classroom might be a new Mother Teresa, or that the newcomer might be a new Nelson Mandela. This indicates that at a fundamental level humanism can only think of education as socialization, as a process of the insertion of newcomers into a preexisting "order" of humanity and, in the case of modern education, as the insertion of newcomers into the preexisting order of modern reason (see Säfström 2003). As a result, humanism is unable to grasp the uniqueness of each individual human being. It can only think of each newcomer as an instance of a human essence that has already been specified and is already known in advance.

Whereas the foregoing considerations amount to an argument against the *desirability* of humanism, there are also questions about the *possibility* of humanism, the possibility to know and articulate the essence of the human being. The question here is not only whether it is possible to achieve *complete* knowledge of the human being or whether there remains always an aspect that cannot be known—an issue raised, for example, by Sigmund Freud. There is also a deeper, philosophical question about the status of knowledge about the human being, more specifically whether it is possible for the human being to be at the same time the source of all knowledge and the object of its own knowledge. Michel Foucault has not only contributed significantly to our understanding of the contradictions inherent in the modern understanding of the human subject in which the human being appears as both a fact among other facts and the transcendental condition of the possibility of all factual knowledge. It was also Foucault who announced the demise and eventual erase of modern man "like a face drawn in sand at the edge of the sea" (Foucault 1973, 387). But as with Levinas and Heidegger, Foucault's proclamation of the end of man was not aimed at the human being as such but at the problematic aspects of a humanist understanding of the human being, and more specifically at the ways in which the modern conception of the human being puts restrictions on what it might mean to be human.

This, then, is what actually is at stake in such phrases as "the end of man" and "the death of the subject" (see Biesta 1998b; Heartfield 2002). They are not meant to denounce human subjectivity or the humanity and dignity of the human being, but are aimed at *humanism,* that is, at the idea that it is possible and desirable to pin down the essence of the human being. The central tenet of the critique of humanism is that humanism has itself become an obstacle to safeguarding the humanity of the human being. Humanism has to be denounced, to quote Levinas once more, not in order to denigrate the human subject but because humanism "is not *sufficiently* human" (Levinas 1981, 128; emphasis added). The challenge then is whether it is possible to approach the question of the humanity of the human being in a different way, a way that is able to overcome the problematic aspects and implications of humanism. This is first of all a challenge for philosophy but, as I have argued, philosophical questions are never merely theoretical questions. The question of what it means to be human touches on *all* our human endeavors and aspirations. It is therefore not only a very practical question but also a very urgent question in a world that continues to be troubled by competing claims about what it means to lead a human life. For all these reasons the challenge to overcome humanism is also a crucial challenge for education—if it is conceded, that is, that there is a meaningful difference between education and socialization; if it is conceded, in other words, that education is more than the simple insertion of the human individual into a preexisting order, that it entails a responsibility for the uniqueness of each individual human being.

In the chapters that follow I explore how we might understand and approach education after the death of the subject. I explore, in other words, what education might look like if it is no longer informed by or based on a humanist under-standing of human subjectivity. On the one hand I discuss in more detail why and how humanism is a problem for education; on the other hand I try to develop a different way to understand and approach education, one, as I mentioned, that sees the question of the humanity of the human being as a radically *open* question, a question that can only be an-swered by engaging in education rather than as a question that needs to be answered *before* we can engage in education. I am particularly interested in providing an alternative for the modern understanding of education in which education is understood in terms of the "production" of the rational autonomous person and in which the educator is seen as a midwife whose task it is to release the rational potential of the human being. This is not to suggest that I am in any way against rationality. It only means that I do not think that rationality can or should be the measure of humanity, or that rationality can be understood outside of the confines of human history.

The approach that I present in this book might be under-stood as a reversal of the traditional way of thinking about education. I argue that we should not approach education from the point of view of an educator trying to produce or release something. Instead I argue that we should focus on the ways in which the new beginning of each and every in-dividual can come "into presence." At first sight this might look like a version of child-centred pedagogy. It is, however, anything but that, because, as I argue in this book, we can only come into presence in a world populated by others who are not like us. The "world," understood as a world of plurality and difference, is not only the *necessary* condition under which human beings can come into presence; it is at the very same time a *troubling* condition, one that makes education an inherently *difficult* process. The role of the educator in all this is not that of a technician or a midwife, but has to be understood in terms of a responsibility for the "coming into the world" of unique, singular beings, and a responsibility for the world as a world of plurality and difference.

In the six chapters that follow I develop this line of thinking in the following way. I begin, in Chapter 1, by placing the discussion in a wider, contemporary context. I show that the language of education seems to have been almost completely replaced by a language of learning. I argue that something has been lost in the transition from "education" to "learning" and that, as a result, many who are currently engaged in education—either as students or as educators—lack a language that can help them understand the complex and difficult character of educational processes and relationships. I explore what constitutes an educational relationship and, through this, provide an outline of a different way to understand and approach education. In the next four chapters I develop the different aspects of this alternative way to understand and approach education in more detail. In Chapter 2 I focus on the critique of humanism and the claims about the end of man and the death of the subject. I argue that rather than trying to find an answer to the question of *what* the human subject is, what its essence and nature are, we should ask a different question, namely, where the human subject, as a unique, singular individual, comes "into presence." I discuss different ways in which "coming into presence" might be understood, and emphasize the social and ethical dimensions of "coming into presence." One important conclusion of this chapter is that we can only come into presence in a world populated by others who are not like us, a world of plurality and difference. In Chapter 3 I continue this argument with an exploration of how we should understand the community in which individuals can come into presence. Such a community, so I argue, is a community that is not constituted by a common identity, but rather exists as a community of radical plurality and difference. In such a community-without-community we can only relate to each other through responsibility, and it is through relationships of responsibility that we are constituted as unique, singular beings. In Chapter 4 I examine in more detail what this implies for and asks from education. I argue that we can only come into the world if others can come into the world as well, which means that our coming into the world is dependent on the existence of plurality and difference. This, however, makes education an inherently difficult if not contradictory process—in the chapter I call this the deconstructive nature of education. I explore how this difficulty should be understood and how it can have a proper place in education. In Chapter 5 I focus in on the question of educational responsibility, and more specifically on the question of the creation of "worldly spaces," spaces of plurality and difference that are a necessary condition for the coming into presence of unique, singular beings. Through a comparison of education with architecture I explore what it means to build a worldly space. I conclude that educational responsibility entails a double duty: a duty for education and for its undoing. In Chapter 6 I show in what ways the approach to education that I have presented in the previous chapters makes a difference for the way in which we understand and approach democratic education. I argue against the idea of democratic education as a process of the production of the democratic person and suggest, instead, an approach that focuses on the ways in which human beings can act, can come into the world as a world of plurality and difference. On the basis of this I offer three new questions for democratic education, questions that do not focus on the education of the democratic person, but ask about the conditions under which action is possible in schools and in society, and about what can be learned from having been or not having been able to act. I conclude the book with a plea for a pedagogy of interruption.

Notes

1. The tradition of *Bildung* is strongly rooted in Continental educational theory and practice, which makes it difficult to provide

an adequate translation of the concept of *Bildung* into English. Although *Bildung* is sometimes translated as "edification" and even as "liberal education," I have decided to use the original German word. For a discussion on the ways in which *Bildung* can be understood in relation to educational traditions in the English-speaking world, see Cleary and Hogan 2001; Biesta 2002a; Biesta 2002b; Løvlie et al., 2003.

2. Levinas considers Heidegger's "discovery" of the difference between the essence or nature of man (man as a being) and man's being or existing (the Being of man) a major breakthrough in Western philosophy (Levinas 1985, 40). This is why he thinks of Heidegger's *Sein und Zeit* (*Being and Time*) as "one of the finest books in the history of philosophy" (Levinas 1985, 37) and of the analysis of the Being of the human being in this book as "extremely brilliant" (Levinas 1985, 39). (He also notes, however, that in order to express his admiration for *Sein und Zeit*, he always tries "to relive the ambiance of those readings when 1933 was still unthinkable" (Levinas 1985, 38). But although Levinas agrees with Heidegger's "diagnosis," he fundamentally disagrees with his "solution," that is, with his designation of man as "the shepherd of Being" (Heidegger 1993 [1947], 234). As a matter of fact, Levinas lists the "ambitious philosophical enterprise in aid of thought and against pure calculation, but subordinating the human to the anonymous gains of Being and, despite its "Letters on Humanism," bringing understanding to Hitlerism itself" (Levinas 1990, 281) as one of the other inhumanities of the twentieth century.

1

Against Learning

Reclaiming a Language for Education in an Age of Learning

Why does language matter to education? If we were to think of language only as a description of reality, there wouldn't be too much to say in response to this question. In that case education simply "is" and language simply describes "what is." Description is, however, only one function of language—and itself a problematic one. Language is not simply a mirror of reality. At least since Dewey and Wittgenstein we know that language is a practice, that it is something we do. And at least since Foucault we know that linguistic and discursive practices delineate—and perhaps we can even say constitute—what can be seen, what can be said, what can be known, what can be thought, and, ultimately, what can be done. Just as language makes some ways of saying and doing possible, it makes other ways of saying and doing difficult and sometimes even impossible. This is an important reason why language matters to education, because the language—or languages—available to education influence to a large extent what can be said and done and also what cannot be said and done.

In this chapter I focus on the way in which the language available to educators has undergone a transformation over the past two decades. I argue that the language of *education* has largely been replaced by a language of *learning.* Although this "new language of learning" has made it possible to express ideas and insights that were rather difficult to articulate by means of the language of education, other aspects of our understanding of what education is or should be about have become far more difficult to articulate. Something has been lost in the shift from the language of education to the language of learning. It is for this reason that I wish to argue that there is a need to reclaim a language *of* education *for* education. To do so, however, cannot simply mean a return to the language or languages that were used in the past. In a sense the task before us is to *reinvent* a language for education—a language that is responsive to the theoretical and practical challenges we are faced with today.

Many educators, past and present, have taken inspiration from an *emancipatory* language of education. There is a long tradition that focuses on education as a process of *individual* emancipation conceived as a trajectory from childhood to adulthood, from dependence to independence, from heteronomy to autonomy. Critical educators have helped us to see that there is no individual emancipation without *societal* emancipation. Notwithstanding the difference in emphasis, both traditions are intimately connected with the Enlightenment idea of emancipation through rational understanding and with the humanist framework in which rationality is seen as both the essence and destiny of the human being. This, as I have shown in the prologue, is expressed in the idea that the aim of education is to reach a state of *rational autonomy.* We now live in an era in which we are beginning to see that there is not *one* rationality but that there are many—an era that we could call postmodern or postcolonial. We now also live in an era in which we are beginning to see that cognition, knowledge, is only one way to relate to the natural and social world, and not necessarily the most fruitful, important, or liberating one. The political and ecological crises that we are witnessing today are an indication that the worldview that underlies the emancipatory language of education might have reached its exhaustion. The most important question for us today is no longer how we can rationally master the natural and social world. The most important question today is how we can respond responsibly to, and how we can live peacefully with what and with whom is other (see, e.g., Säfström and Biesta 2001).

In this chapter I wish to make a contribution to the development of a language of education that is responsive to these challenges. I will suggest building blocks for a language that puts an emphasis on educational relationships, on trust, and on responsibility, while acknowledging the inherently *difficult* character of education. In later chapters I will explore these dimensions in more detail.

The New Language of Learning

One of the most remarkable changes that has taken place in the theory and practice of education over the past two decades has been the rise of the concept of "learning" and the subsequent decline of the concept of "education." Teaching has become redefined as supporting or facilitating learning, just as education is now often described as providing learning opportunities or learning experiences. Pupils and students have become learners, and adult education has become adult learning. In England and Wales, Further Education and Adult Education have officially been redesignated as the Learning and Skills Sector. And governments around the world no longer plea for recurrent or permanent education but stress the need for lifelong learning and the creation of a learning society. "Learning" has also become a favorite concept in national and international policy documents, as can be seen in such titles as *Lifelong Learning for All* (OECD 1996), *The Learning Age: A Renaissance for a New Britain* (DfEE 1998), and *Learning to Succeed* (DfEE 1999). The UK now even has an Internet-based provision for everyone who wants to learn, called *learndirect®*, set up by the University for Industry and aimed at transforming the UK into a learning society. The *learndirect®* Web site advertises its provision as follows:

> Welcome to **learndirect**.
> **learndirect** is a brand new form of learning that's for everyone!
> **learndirect** learning is designed with you in mind. Our courses are computer-based but don't let that bother you! The easiest way to get started is to go to one of the many **learndirect** centres around the country. Our friendly staff will be on hand to help you out. You don't need any experience—we'll take you through your learning step by step. (http://www.learndirect.co.uk/personal [accessed March 10, 2003])

The following excerpt from a document on lifelong learning published by the European Commission provides another clear example of what I propose to call the "new language of learning."

> Placing learners and learning at the centre of education and training methods and processes is by no means a new idea, but in practice, the established framing of pedagogic practices in most formal contexts has privileged teaching rather than learning.... In a high-technology knowledge society, this kind of teaching-learning loses efficacy: learners must become proactive and more autonomous, prepared to renew their knowledge continuously and to respond constructively to changing constellations of problems and contexts. The teacher's role becomes one of accompaniment, facilitation, mentoring, support and guidance in the service of learners' own efforts to access, use and ultimately create knowledge. (Commission of the European Communities 1998, 9, quoted in Field 2000, 136)

Although the concept of "learning" has become almost omnipresent in contemporary educational discourse, it is important to see that the new language of learning is *not* the outcome of a particular process or the expression of a single underlying agenda. It rather should be understood as the result of a combination of different, partly even contradictory trends and developments, which suggests that the new language of learning is more an effect of a range of events than the intended outcome of a particular program or agenda. There are at least four trends that, in one way or another, have contributed to the rise of the new language of learning.

1. *New Theories of Learning.* One influential trend can be found in the field of the psychology of learning and concerns the emergence of constructivist and sociocultural theories of learning (see, e.g., Fosnot 1996; Lave and Wenger 1991). Such theories have challenged the idea that learning is the passive intake of information and have instead argued that knowledge and understanding are actively constructed by the learner, often in cooperation with other learners. This has shifted the attention away from the activities of the teachers to the activities of the students. As a result, learning has become much more central in the understanding of the process of education. Notions such as "scaffolding" have provided a perspective in which teaching can easily be redefined as supporting and facilitating learning.

2. *Postmodernism.* The impact of postmodernism on educational theory and practice has also contributed to the rise of the new language of learning. Over the past two decades many authors have argued that the project of education is a thoroughly modern project, intimately connected to the heritage of the Enlightenment (see, e.g., Usher and Edwards 1994). The postmodern doubt about the possibility and viability of the project of modernity has therefore raised fundamental questions about the modern configuration of education, particularly with regard to the idea that educators can liberate and emancipate their students by imparting rationality and critical thinking. If, as has for example been

argued by the German educationalist Hermann Giesecke (1985), postmodernism implies the end of education, what can be left but learning?

3. *The "Silent Explosion" of Adult Learning.* The rise of the new language of learning is not only the effect of theoretical and conceptual shifts. There is also the simple fact that more and more people nowadays spend more and more of their time and money on all kinds of different forms of learning, inside and increasingly also outside of the formal settings of established educational institutions. There is not only conclusive evidence that the volume and level of participation in formal adult education has increased, there is also a rapidly growing market for nonformal forms of learning, such as in fitness centers and sports clubs, through self-help manuals, the Internet, videos, CDs, DVDs, et cetera. One of the most significant characteristics of what John Field (2000) has referred to as the "silent explosion of learning," is that the new learning is far more *individualistic,* in terms of its form and its content and purpose. Field notices that many adult learners nowadays are struggling with themselves, for example, with their body, their relationships, or their identity. The individualistic and individualized nature of the activities in which new adult learners are engaged helps to understand why the word *learning* has become such an appropriate concept to use to describe these activities.

4. *The Erosion of the Welfare State.* The rise of the new language of learning can also be related to wider socioeconomic and political developments, particularly the erosion of the welfare state and the rise of the market ideology of neoliberalism. One of the key ideas underlying the welfare state is the principle of the redistribution of wealth so that provisions such as health care, social security, and education can be made available to all citizens and not just to those who can afford it. Although much of this is still in place in many countries (albeit with increasing levels of public-private partnerships or even full-blown privatization), the relationship between governments and citizens has in many cases changed from

a political relationship to an economic relationship: a relationship between the state as provider of public services and the taxpayer as the consumer of state provision. "Value for money" has become a guiding principle in the transactions between the state and its taxpayers. This way of thinking lies at the basis of the emergence of a culture of accountability that has resulted in tight systems of inspection and control and ever more prescriptive educational protocols. It is also the logic behind voucher systems and the idea that parents, as the consumers of the education of their children, should ultimately decide what should be offered in schools (for a critical analysis of the demise of education as a public good, see, for example, Englund 1994; Apple 2000; Biesta 2004a). This way of thinking introduces a logic that focuses almost exclusively on the user, or consumer, of educational provision. What could be a more suitable name for such a consumer than "the learner"?

If this suffices as an indication of why the new language of learning might have emerged—and I wish to emphasize once more that these developments are not the outcome of a single underlying agenda and that they are not all necessarily problematic or bad—the question to ask next is what the impact of the new language of learning has been on the discourse and practice of education. What is the problem with the new language of learning? What is it that can be said by means of the new language of learning and, more importantly, what is it that can no longer be said by means of this language? Could there be a reason to be against "learning"?

Against Learning?

The main problem with the new language of learning is that it has facilitated a redescription of the process of education in terms of an *economic transaction,* that is, a transaction in which (1) the learner is the (potential) consumer, the one who has certain "needs," in which (2) the teacher, the educator, or the educational institution is seen as the provider, that is, the one who is there to meet the needs of the learner, and where (3) education itself becomes a commodity—a "thing"—to be provided or delivered by the teacher or educational institution and to be consumed by the learner. This is the logic that lies behind the idea that educational institutions and individual educators should be flexible, that they should respond to the needs of the learners, that they should give their learners value for money, and perhaps even that they should operate on the principle that the learner/customer is always right. This is clearly the world of *learndirect*®, in which "you don't need any experience," where computer-based learning shouldn't "bother you," and where "our friendly staff will be on hand to help you out." It is also the logic that demands that educators and educational institutions should be accountable, since what ultimately constitutes the relationship between the learner/consumer and the educator/provider is the payments learners make, either direct or, in the case of state-funded education, through taxation.

In one respect it does make sense to look at the process of education in these terms, at least, that is, in order to redress the imbalances of a situation in which education has been mainly provider-led and inflexible. Access to education has, after all, everything to do with such basic things as being able to attend school, college, or university, and traditionally those groups who were not able to organize their lives around the requirements and timetables of educational institutions were simply excluded from many educational opportunities. This is why evening classes, open universities, and flexible and distance learning are so important. It is also the main reason why educational institutions and individual educators should indeed respond to the needs of the learners. To think of students as learners and learners as customers who want value for money can indeed be helpful in achieving equal educational opportunities for all.

The more fundamental question, however, is whether education itself can be understood—and should be understood—in economic terms, that is, as a situation where the learner has certain needs and it is the business of the educator to meet those needs. I believe, following Feinberg (2001), that this is *not* the case and that it is for precisely this reason that the comparison between an economic and an educational relationship falls short. Why is this so?

In the case of economic transactions we can, in principle, assume that consumers know what their needs are and that they know what they want. (The "in principle" is important here, because we know all too well how consumers' needs are manufactured by the advertising industry.) Is this also a valid assumption in the case of education? It might seem that most parents know very well what they want from the school to which they send their children. But this is only true at a very general level—and might perhaps only be true because of the existence of strong cultural expectations about why children should go to school and what can be expected from schools and schooling. But most parents do not—or not yet—send their children to school with a detailed list of what they want the teacher to do. Like: "Dear Miss, Please give Mary thirty minutes of mathematics instruction using method A, followed by fifteen minutes of remedial teaching, and after that, please give her twenty minutes of religious education, and a bit of interaction with the other children in her class as well." Parents generally send their children to school because they want them to be educated, but it is up to the professional judgment and expertise of the teacher to make decisions about what this particular child actually needs. Here lies a fundamental difference between the economic or market model and the professional model. As Feinberg explains: "In market models consumers are supposed to know what they need, and producers bid in price and quality to satisfy them. In professional models the producer not only services a need, but also defines it.... Sam goes to his physician complaining of a headache. Is it an aspirin or brain surgery that he needs? Only the doctor knows" (Feinberg 2001, 403).

Would this situation be different in the case of adult learners? Presumably not. Adults might on average be more able to articulate what they want from education and might hence be better able to define their educational needs. But there are many cases in which adults engage in education specifically to find out what it is that they really want or need. We also shouldn't forget the many accounts of adults for whom engaging in education was literally a life-transforming event, an experience through which they not only came to know what it was they really wanted or needed, but through which they also found a new sense of self. This is not to suggest that finding a new sense of self or a new identity is always a positive experience. Finding a new identity means giving up an old identity, and quite often there is no way back, as is evidenced in such classics as Willy Russell's *Educating Rita* and George Bernard Shaw's *Pygmalion*.

To think of education as an economic transaction, as a process of meeting the needs of the learner—something that is made possible by the new language of learning—is therefore first of all problematic because it misconstrues both the role of the learner and the role of the educational professional in the educational relationship. It forgets that a major reason for engaging in education is precisely to find out what it is that one actually wants or needs. It also forgets that educational professionals have a crucial role to play in the process of needs definition, because a major part of their professional expertise lies precisely there; a role that precisely distinguishes them from shop assistants whose only task it is to deliver the goods to the customer.

The idea that education should be about meeting the predefined needs of the learner is also problematic because it suggests a framework in which the only questions that can meaningfully be asked about education are *technical* questions, that is, questions about the efficiency and the effectiveness of the educational *process*. The more important questions about the content and purpose of education become virtually impossible to ask, other, that is, than in response to the needs of the learner. Since it is assumed that the learner knows or should know what he or she wants to learn and why he or she wants to learn it, questions about the content and purpose of education not only become wholly *individualized,* but on a wider scale they can become subject to the forces of the market. One effect of this is that, in order to attract learners, learning itself has to be depicted as easy, attractive, exciting, and whatnot more—which is precisely the message of *learndirect®,* the "brand new form of learning," for which "you don't need any experience," and where the use of computers "shouldn't bother you."

There might well be significant areas in which it should indeed be up to the individual learner to decide about the content and purpose of his or her learning. My point here is not to say that only some learning should count as legitimate and respectable. But I do wish to argue that questions about the content and purpose of learning should first of all be seen as important educational questions in that gaining an understanding of what it is one wants or needs is itself an important learning experience. I am therefore also saying that these questions should be seen as social and interpersonal questions and not simply as questions of individual preference. Questions about who we are and who we want to become through education, although of immense importance to ourselves, are always also questions about our relationships with others and about our place in the social fabric. On a wider scale, questions about the content and purpose of education are therefore fundamentally *political* questions. To leave an answer to these questions to the forces of the market—and we all know how manipulative markets can be in order to secure their own future—deprives us of the opportunity to have a democratic say in the educational renewal of society.

There are, therefore, two objections against the new language of learning or, to be more precise, against a line of thinking that is made possible by the new language of learning. One problem is that the new language of learning facilitates an *economic* understanding of the process of education, one in which the learner is supposed to know what he or she wants, and where a provider is simply there to meet the needs of the learner (or, in more crude terms: *to satisfy the customer*). I have shown how such a depiction misconstrues the dynamics of educational relationships. The other problem with the logic of the new language of learning is that it makes it very difficult to raise questions about the content and purpose of education, other than in terms of what "the consumer" or "the market" wants. This, as I have argued, poses a threat to educational professionalism and ultimately also undermines the democratic deliberation about the ends of education.

For these reasons I believe that we should be extremely cautious in using the language of learning. This is not only because such usage might undermine our own professionalism as educators, but also because it might erode and open, democratic discussion about the content and purpose of education. Our attitude can, however, not simply be a negative one. We need to reclaim—or rather reinvent—a language of education that can serve as an alternative for the language of learning. To this task I will turn now.

From Learning to Education: What Constitutes an Educational Relationship?

I have argued that we shouldn't understand the educational relationship as an economic relationship, that is, as a relationship between a provider and a consumer. But what, then, constitutes an educational relationship? And what kind of language would be appropriate to capture what is special about educational relationships? My answer to this question centers around three interlocking concepts: trust, violence, and responsibility, or, to be more precise: trust without ground, transcendental violence, and responsibility without knowledge.

Trust (without Ground)

Where does education begin? It might, indeed, begin with a learner who wishes to learn something, who seeks knowledge, skills, qualifications, change, or adventure, and who seeks a way to learn this and perhaps even someone to learn from. We can of course try to put this process into neat boxes. The learner knows what she wants to learn, so the provider must make sure that it is precisely this—nothing more and nothing less—that the learner will learn. Hence learning contracts, hence accountability, hence inspection and control, and hence *learndirect®*—the "brand new form of learning," which is designed "with you in mind."

Yet even if one engages in very neatly organized forms of learning, there is always a *risk.* Not only is there a risk that you do not learn what you wanted to learn (in which case you can always sue the provider). There is also the risk that you will learn things that you couldn't have imagined that you would learn or that you couldn't have imagined that you would have wanted to learn. And there is the risk that you will learn something that you didn't want to learn—something about yourself, for example. To engage in learning always entails the risk that learning might have an impact on you, that learning might change you. This means that education only begins when the learner is willing to take a risk.

One way of putting this is to say that one of the constituents of the educational relationship is *trust.* Why are risk and trust connected? This is fundamentally because trust is about those situations in which you do not know and cannot know what will happen. Trust is by its very nature without ground, because if one's trust were grounded, that is, if one *knew* what was going to happen or how the person they have put their trust in would act and respond, trust would not be needed. Trust would have been replaced by calculation. Trust, however, is about what is *incalculable.* This is not to suggest, of course, that trust should be blind. It is only meant to highlight the fact that trust *structurally* and not accidentally entails a moment of risk. To negate or deny the risk involved in engaging in education is to miss a crucial dimension of education. To suggest that education can be and should be risk free, that learners don't run any risk by engaging in education, or that learning outcomes can be known and specified in advance, is a misrepresentation of what education is about.

It could be argued that the validity of the foregoing argument depends on how one defines learning and also on the kind of learning one engages in. After all, not all learning entails a similar amount of risk, and some forms of learning might be quite predictable in their outcomes. Although I am inclined to argue that all learning might lead to unexpected change and that for this reason there is no fundamental difference among driving lessons, an art history course, learning how to weld, or learning how to write, it is indeed important to look at the way in which we define and understand learning itself. This brings me to the second aspect of my answer to the question of what constitutes an education relationship.

(Transcendental) Violence

What is learning? Learning theorists of both an individualistic and a sociocultural bent have developed a range of accounts of how learning—or more precisely, how the *process* of learning—takes place. Although they differ in their description and explanation of the process, for example, by focusing on processes in the brain or legitimate peripheral participation, many of such accounts assume that learning has to do with the acquisition of something "external," something that existed before the act of learning and that, as a result of learning, becomes the possession of the learner. This is what many people have in mind when they say that someone has learned something.

We can, however, also look at learning from a different angle and see it as a *response*. Instead of seeing learning as an attempt to acquire, to master, to internalize, or any other possessive metaphors we can think of, we might see learning as a reaction to a disturbance, as an attempt to reorganize and reintegrate as a result of disintegration. We might look at learning as a response to what is other and different, to what challenges, irritates, or even disturbs us, rather than as the acquisition of something we want to possess. Both ways of looking at learning—learning as acquisition and learning as responding—might be equally valid, depending, that is, on the situation in which we raise questions about the definition of learning. But as I will argue in more detail in subsequent chapters, the second conception of learning is *educationally* the more significant, if it is conceded that education is not just about the transmission of knowledge, skills, and values, but is concerned with the individuality, subjectivity, or person-hood of the student, with their "coming into the world" as unique, singular beings.

While learning as acquisition is about getting more and more, learning as responding is about showing who you are and where you stand. Coming into the world is not some-thing individuals can do on their own. This is first of all for the obvious reason that in order to come into the world one needs a world, and this world is a world inhabited by others who are not like us. Coming into the world also isn't something that we should understand as an act or decision of a pre-social individual. This is first of all because a case can be made that the very structure of our subjectivity, the very structure of who we are, is thoroughly social. Even when uttering a simple word like *I* we are already making use of a language that in a very fundamental sense is not of our own making, or of our own possession (see Derrida 1998). But it is also, as I will discuss in more detail in Chapters 2 and 3, because what makes us into a unique, singular being—me, and not you—is precisely to be found in the way in which we respond to the other, to the question of the other and to the other as question (see Levinas 1989a; 1998; Biesta 2003a).

If we look at education from this angle it becomes clear that one of the key educational responsibilities is that of providing opportunities for individuals to come into the world. What might it mean to provide such opportunities? It requires first and foremost the creation of situations in which learners are able and are allowed to respond. This not only means that there must be something to respond to—a curriculum, for example, but not a curriculum as the content that needs to be acquired but as the practice that allows for particular responses (see Biesta 2005). It also requires that educators and educational institutions show an interest in the thoughts and feelings of their students and allow them to respond in their own, unique ways. This certainly has implications for pedagogy and for the social organization of learning. What it does *not* mean, however, is that any response will suffice and should simply be accepted. Coming into the world is definitely *not* about self-expression. It is about entering the social fabric and is therefore thoroughly relational (see Sidorkin and Bingham 2004). It is about responding to and therefore also being responsible for what and who is other—a theme I develop in more detail in Chapters 2 and 3. To respond is therefore as much about activity, about saying and doing, as it is about passivity: listening, waiting, being attentive, creating space (see Biesta 2001).

Teachers and other educators not only have a crucial task in creating the opportunities and a climate in which students can actually respond, they also have a task in challenging their students to respond by confronting them with what and who is other and by posing such fundamental questions as "What do you think about it?," "Where do you stand?," and "How will you respond?" (see Rancière 1991, 36; see also Masschelein 1998, 144; Biesta 1998a). There is no doubt that these are very *difficult* questions—and I return to the question of how difficult education actually should be in

Chapter 4. Yet these questions are also in a very fundamental sense *educational* questions, because they challenge students to show who they are and where they stand. In doing so, these questions make it possible for students to come into the world as unique, individual beings.

If asking such difficult questions is a central and necessary aspect of educational relationships, then it is important to acknowledge that such relationships are not necessarily easy or pleasant. By asking the difficult questions that allow students to come into the world, we challenge and possibly disturb who and where our students are. This means that education entails a *violation* of the sovereignty of the student. Derrida refers to this violation as "transcendental violence" (see Derrida 1978). Education is a form of violence in that it interferes with the sovereignty of the subject by asking difficult questions and creating difficult encounters. Yet it is this violation that makes the coming into the world of unique, singular beings possible—which is why Derrida refers to it as *transcendental* violence, where "transcendental" refers to that which needs to occur in order to make something possible. To highlight that education entails a violation of the sovereignty of the student is, of course, not to suggest that education should be violent. It is only meant as a reminder that as educators we are always interfering in the lives of our students and that this interference can have a deep, transforming, and even disturbing impact on our students—which is, of course, a far cry from the world of *learndirect*®, in which learning is depicted as "nice and easy" and without any risks.

Responsibility (without Knowledge)

If this is what constitutes an educational relationship and makes education possible, then it is immediately clear that educators carry an immense responsibility. This responsibility is more than a responsibility for the "quality" of teaching or for successfully meeting the needs of the learner or the targets of the institution. If education is about creating opportunities for students to come into the world, and if it is about asking the difficult questions that make this possible, then it becomes clear that the first responsibility of the educator is a responsibility for the *subjectivity* of the student, for that which allows the student to be a unique, singular being. Taking responsibility for the singularity of the student, for the uniqueness of this particular student, is not something that has to do with calculation. It is not that we first need to know everything about our students before we can take responsibility for them. Neither is it the case that we can only take responsibility for our students if we know what this responsibility actually entails, that is, if we were to know what will actually happen in the future as a result of our educational efforts and interventions. It rather belongs to the very structure of responsibility that we do not know what we take responsibility for—if *taking* is the right word in the first place. In this sense responsibility is *unlimited*, because, as Derrida reminds us, a limited responsibility is just an excuse to credit oneself with good conscience. He writes:

> When the path is clear and given, when a certain knowledge opens up the way in advance, the decision is already made, it might as well be said that there is none to make; irresponsibly, and in good conscience, one simply applies or implements a program.... It makes of action the applied consequence, the simple application of a knowledge or know-how. It makes of ethics and politics a technology. No longer of the order of practical reason or decision, it begins to be irresponsible. (Derrida 1992, 41, 45)

To engage in *educational* relationships, to *be* a teacher or to *be* an educator, therefore implies a responsibility for something (or better, someone) that we do not know and cannot know. This is why *responsibility without knowledge* should be seen as the third dimension of what constitutes an educational relationship—and in Chapter 5, I discuss in more detail what this responsibility entails.

For Education

In this chapter I have examined the new language of learning. I have argued that the emergence of the new language of learning should be understood as the unintended outcome of a range of different developments. These developments are, as such, not all bad. New theories of learning have definitely had a positive impact on educational practices; the postmodern critique of modern education has effectively exposed authoritarian structures and practices; and the actual increase in learning, the "silent explosion," has indeed opened up many new opportunities for learning. I am less optimistic about the rise of neoliberalism (see also Biesta 2004a), and it seems that the new language of learning fits the neoliberal framework rather well. I have argued that to think of education as an economic transaction not only misconstrues the role of the learner and the educator in the educational relationship, it also results in a situation in which questions about the content and purpose of education become subject to the forces of the market instead of being the concern of professional judgment and democratic deliberation.

Although the new language of learning has been beneficial in some respects, it has made it far more difficult to ask *educational* questions about education—which shows why language does matter to education. In the second half of the chapter I have therefore tried to make clear what it means to ask such questions. I have done this through an exploration of the constituents of educational relationships and have focused on the way in which through such relationships individuals as unique, singular beings can come into the world. By emphasizing how educational relationships are constituted by trust without ground, transcendental violence, and responsibility

without knowledge, I have begun to outline a different way
to understand education, one that isn't based on a particular
truth about the human subject and doesn't see education as
a process of the "production" of a particular kind of subjectivity, particularly not the rational autonomous subject of
modern education. In the next five chapters I present and
discuss this approach in more detail. In Chapter 2 I suggest
a way in which we might be able to overcome humanism in
education by moving from the question of what the human
subject is to the question of where the human subject comes
into presence. I argue that we can only come into presence
in a world populated by other human beings who are not
like us. In Chapter 3 I explore this idea in more detail by
examining the relationship between education, community,
and responsibility. In Chapter 4 I discuss the difficult nature
of educational processes and relationships, and in Chapter 5
I turn to the question of the responsibility of the educator. In
Chapter 6 I show how this way to understand and approach
makes a difference in the theory and practice of democratic
education.

2

Coming into Presence

Education after the Death of the Subject

Once upon a time—modern time—there lived a subject. This subject was seen as the autonomous, pre-social, and transhistoric source of truth and rationality and of its own identity. It was the point from which the universe could be moved. We have been told that this subject is no longer with us: It has been decentered, it has reached its end, it has died. And yet this death of the subject "which was proudly proclaimed *urbi et orbi* not so long ago" (Laclau 1995, 93) has been succeeded by a new and widespread interest in questions about subjectivity and identity. As Ernesto Laclau has suggested, the death of the Subject with a capital *S* may well have been the precondition of this renewed interest. Perhaps, as he writes, it is "the very impossibility of referring any longer the concrete and finite expressions of a multifarious subjectivity to a transcendental center that makes it possible to concentrate our attention on the multiplicity itself" (Laclau 1995,

93). The subject thus seems to have moved from the center of the universe to the center of contemporary discussions and practical and political interest. What we are therefore witnessing today, as Laclau puts it, is "the death of the death of the subject," the "re-emergence of the subject as a result of its own death" (Laclau 1995, 94).

In this chapter I explore some of the implications of the so-called death of the subject for education. In the first part of the chapter I discuss what actually is at stake in the discussion. Through a reading of Foucault I show that the discussion about the death of the subject—or in Foucault's phrase, the end of man—should be understood as a critique of *humanism,* a critique, that is, of the idea that it is possible to define the essence of what it is to be human. I argue that one of the main problems with the strategy of humanism is that it can only understand the human being as a "what"—a "thing"—but never as a "who." Humanism can only see individual human beings as instances of some more general essence, but can never think of the human being in its singularity and uniqueness. In the second part of the chapter I suggest an approach to the question of human subjectivity that is focused on the question of where and how the human being as a unique individual "comes into presence." I argue that we come into presence through our relationships with others who are not like us. I also argue that what makes us unique in such relationships, what constitutes us as unique, singular beings, is to be found in the ethical dimension of such relationships.

The Subject of Education

One thing that has become increasingly clear as a result of the discussions on postmodernism and education is the intimate relationships among Enlightenment, modernity, and the educational "project." Robin Usher and Richard Edwards have argued that modern education is the "dutiful child" of the

Enlightenment. It is "the vehicle by which the Enlightenment ideals of critical reason, humanistic individual freedom and benevolent progress are substantiated and realized" (Usher and Edwards 1994, 24). According to Usher and Edwards, the very rationale of the educational process "is founded on the humanist idea of a certain kind of subject who has the inherent potential to become self-motivated and self-directing, a rational subject capable of exercising individual agency" (Usher and Edwards 1994, 24). What is typically modern about this process is that the task of education is understood as one of "bringing out" or helping to realize this potential "so that subjects become fully autonomous and capable of exercising their individual and intentional agency" (Usher and Edwards 1994, 24–25). This is exactly what Immanuel Kant had in mind when he defined Enlightenment as "man's release from his self-incurred tutelage [Unmundigkeit] through the exercise of his own understanding" (Kant 1992, 90).

The idea that education should bring about rational autonomy has influenced educational practices up to the present day, not in the least through the impact of developmental psychology on educational theory and practice. In the work of Jean Piaget, rational autonomy figures as the highest stage—and hence the desirable outcome—of cognitive development, whereas in Lawrence Kohlberg's work, it characterizes the highest stage of moral development. In this way the modern conception of what it means to be human has become part of our ideas about normal human development. This, in turn, has made it possible to identify deviations from the norm, exemplified in ideas about retarded cognitive and moral development, learning difficulties, and special educational needs—ideas that have thoroughly influenced the institutional landscape of education. The notion of rational autonomy also plays a central role in critical approaches to education, particularly through the idea that it is the motor for emancipation (see, e.g., Mollenhauer 1964; McLaren 1997).

Politically the emergence of the modern educational project coincided with the birth of civil society (see Bauman 1992, 3).

Education played a historic role in the shift from the heteronomous determination by God, church, and king to autonomy and self-government, not only because of the suggestion that "Enlightenment-through-education" was *possible,* but even more because of the claim that in order to reach the state of autonomy and self-government, education was *necessary.* In his essay on education Emmanuel Kant proclaimed that human beings can only become human, that is, autonomous beings, through education (see Kant 1982, 697–699).

Philosophically the crossing of the "threshold of our modernity" (Foucault 1973, 319) was supported by a tradition that took the knowing subject—the *ego cogito,* the knowing consciousness—as its point of departure and its foundation. The tradition of the "philosophy of consciousness" found its culmination in Kant's transcendental philosophy in which the knowing consciousness—the "I think" or *"Ich denke"*—was seen as the "highest point to which we must ascribe all employment of the understanding, even the whole of logic, and conformally therewith, transcendental philosophy" (Kant 1929, B134).

Although the tradition of the philosophy of consciousness still occupies a central place in modern philosophy, the idea of the *ego cogito* as foundation and point of departure has been challenged long before the rise of postmodern thought. Hegel already questioned the scheme of the philosophy of consciousness by arguing that the community is not an external force that coerces previously isolated individuals, but that individuals are in some way constituted by the community. In the twentieth century the Hegelian intuition was taken up by such thinkers as Dewey, Mead, Wittgenstein, and Habermas, who all argued against the idea of the *ego cogito* as starting point and foundation and instead gave primacy to intersubjective social practices (Dewey: communication; Mead: symbolic interaction; Wittgenstein: forms of life; Habermas: communicative action).

The step from consciousness to intersubjectivity has effected a crucial shift in Western philosophy, as it has opened up new and different ways to understand subjectivity and, more specifically, to understand the relationship between the subject and other subjects. In the tradition of the philosophy of consciousness it is assumed that my thinking precedes my encounter with the world and, more specifically, that my thinking has epistemological priority over my encounter with the world—a world that includes other subjects. In this scheme the other appears first of all as an object of my consciousness, an object of my experience and knowledge. The intersubjective "turn" in twentieth-century philosophy has questioned the apparent self-evidence of the *ego cogito* and has opened up new avenues for understanding human subjectivity. Although the shift from consciousness to intersubjectivity has provided a frame of reference that makes it possible, in principle, to overcome the problematic relationship with the other that is inherent in the tradition of the philosophy of consciousness (see Wimmer 1988), there is a sense in which this shift is still tied up with the very tradition it seeks to overcome. The problem is this: As long as we keep thinking about intersubjectivity as a new theory or new truth about the human subject—which is implied in such popular notions as man as a relational being, a historically and socially situated being, or a socially constructed being—we continue to rely at the level of theorizing on the totalizing gesture of a consciousness that claims to be able to overlook and know the field in which the subject emerges.

The End of Man

It is here that more recent discussions about the "end of man" and the "death of the subject" represent a different intervention in the tradition of the philosophy of consciousness. Although Michel Foucault is not the only "postmodern" philosopher who has addressed these issues, his work has played a major role in the discussion about the dislocation of the subject. In his book *The Order of Things: An Archaeology of the Human Sciences* (Foucault 1973), Foucault put forward the claim that man as we know him today, that is, as both "an object of knowledge and a subject that knows" (Foucault 1973, 312), is a "recent invention" (Foucault 1973, 386). He locates the emergence of "man" in the epistemic shift from the Classical Age to the Modern Age, a shift that took place at the beginning of the nineteenth century. Foucault argues that in the Classical Age man was just a being among other beings, having its place in the divine order of things. As the belief in this divine order and man's place in it began to break down, the recognition of man's finitude started to emerge. The startling thing about this recognition, Foucault argues, was that it was not lamented as a limitation but, most explicitly in the philosophy of Kant, made into the very condition of possibility of all knowledge. Foucault sees this attempt—a strategy to which he refers as the *analytic of finitude*—as the defining characteristic of the Modern Age. The analytic of finitude received its anthropological articulation in Kant's "empirico-transcendental doublet" (Foucault 1973, 319): man as an empirical being among other beings and man as the transcendental condition of all empirical knowledge. This double-figure marks the "threshold to our modernity" (Foucault 1973, 319).

According to Foucault the modern conception of man was doomed right from the start because of its inherently contradictory character. He shows how modern philosophy was haunted by the difficult if not impossible task to claim simultaneously an identity and a difference between the "positive" (human subjectivity as finite) and the "fundamental" (human subjectivity as the condition of the possibility of all knowledge) (see Foucault 1973, 319). Under the modern *episteme* man appeared (1) as a fact among other facts to be studied empirically, and yet as the transcendental condition of the possibility of all knowledge (for example in Kant's philosophy); (2) as surrounded by what he cannot get clear about, and yet as a potentially lucid cogito, the source of all intelligibility (for example in the work of Husserl and Freud);

and (3) as the product of a long history whose beginning he can never reach and yet, paradoxically, as the source of that very history (for example in Heidegger's work) (see Dreyfus and Raboniw 1983, 31). Even more important—and more controversial—than his claim that man is a recent invention, was the conclusion Foucault drew from his investigations. Foucault concluded that because the emergence of man is bound up with the modern *episteme,* there is every reason to expect the eventual erasure of man "like a face drawn in sand at the edge of the sea" (Foucault 1973, 387).

It has been for this particular phrase that Foucault's work has been taken as the very subversion of human subjectivity. But even a superficial glance at Foucault's arguments shows that what is at stake in the idea of the end of man is *not* the eventual erasure of man "as such," but only the end of a particular, *modern* articulation of human subjectivity. Foucault's claim about the end of man only concerns a particular subject and a particular kind of subjectivity, one that was developed in a particular age under particular circumstances and, so we might add, for particular purposes. This is not to say that Foucault's critique is only aimed at this specific theory of subjectivity so that all problems would be solved once we would come up with a new theory. Foucault's critique is aimed at the more general strategy in which "you first set up a theory of the subject ... and that, beginning from that theory of the subject, you come to pose the question, for example, how such and such a form of knowledge was possible" (Foucault 1991, 10). Foucault's objection concerns any a priori theory of the subject, that is, any theory about the subject that does not take the theorizing activity of that subject itself into account. He argues that because such a theory assumes prior objectification, it cannot be asserted as a basis for analytic work. This does not imply that analytic work should go on without conceptualization. But Foucault warns us that "the conceptualized object is not the single criterion of a good conceptualization" (Foucault 1983, 209).

Foucault's thesis about the end of man is therefore not simply a critique of the self-present and self-presenting *ego cogito* of modern philosophy. It is addressed at the more general strategy of modern philosophy in which the basic philosophical question is considered to be an *anthropological* question, that is, the question "What is man?" (see Foucault 1973, 340–341). Foucault's critique is aimed at the anthropological configuration of modern philosophy in which "the pre-critical analysis of what man is in his essence becomes the analytic of everything that can, in general, be presented to man's experience" (Foucault 1973, 341). It is aimed at the "anthropological sleep" (Foucault 1973, 340), which Kant induced in modern philosophy. It is aimed, in short, at the humanistic foundations of modernity (see also Simons 1995, 42–50).

It is precisely at this point that Foucault's critique of humanism echoes the work of Heidegger and Levinas. As I have shown in the preface to this book, Heidegger's critique of humanism is aimed at the fact that humanism is *metaphysical*, in that it is "either grounded in metaphysics or is itself made to be the ground of one" (Heidegger 1993 [1947], 225). This makes it impossible to address the question of the humanity of the human being in an adequate way, because "[e]very determination of the essence of man … already presupposes an interpretation of beings without asking about the truth of Being" (Heidegger 1993 [1947], 225–226). The problem with humanism, in Heidegger's words, therefore is that it "does not set the *humanitas* of man high enough" (Heidegger 1993 [1947], 233–234). The problem with humanism, as Levinas has put it, is that it is not *sufficiently* human. For Levinas this has everything to do with the fact that humanism can only think of the individual subject as an instance of a more general human essence. Humanism can only understand the human being "within a framework of his belonging to a genus—the human genus" (Levinas 1998b, 189). As a consequence, the subject can never appear in its "uniqueness" (Levinas 1998b, 189), it can never appear in its singularity (Levinas 1998a,

26), that is, as *this* individual. What Foucault helps us to see is that the way out of this predicament does not lie in a new *theory* of the subject. It rather requires a new *approach* to the question of human subjectivity.

In Foucault's own work the word *approach* is taken quite literally. He argues that what is needed to overcome humanism is not a new doctrine or a new theory, but a different attitude or philosophical *ethos* (see Foucault 1984, 42). Foucault refers to this ethos as a critical and historical "ontology of ourselves" and sees it as a thoroughly practical mode of critique that takes the form of a possible *transgression* (see Foucault 1984, 105). He defines transgression as "a historical investigation into the events that have led us to constitute ourselves and to recognize ourselves as subjects of what we are doing, thinking, saying [in order] to separate out from the contingency that has made us what we are, the possibility of no longer being, doing, or thinking what we are, do, or think" (Foucault 1984, 105). This implies that transgression is thoroughly experimental. The "work done at the limits of ourselves" must not only open up a realm of historical inquiry, but must also put itself to the test (see Foucault 1984, 105). It has to be conceived as a historical, practical, and nonuniversal test of the limits that are imposed on us, and "an experiment with the possibility of going beyond them" (Foucault 1984, 108)—although it should be kept in mind that to go beyond limits does not mean to move to a realm that is limitless. At stake is the development of *different* ways of "being, doing or thinking what we are, do, or think."

This shows that although the way to overcome humanism is not to be found in a new theory or truth about human subjectivity, we shouldn't stop thinking. What is needed, so we might say, is not so much a new answer to the question of what the human subject *is,* as a new way of formulating this question. In what follows I suggest that one way of doing this is to shift from the question of *what* the subject is to the question of where the subject, as a unique, singular being, *comes into presence.*

Who Comes after the Subject?

In his contribution to the book *Who Comes after the Subject?* (Cadava et al. 1991), Gérard Granel argues that the subject of modern philosophy, either in the form of "transcendental *subjectivity*" or as a "historical *subjectum*," has never been thought of as a "who" but has always been approached as a "what," as a thing (Granel 1991, 148). Whereas the question of *what* the subject is asks for a definition of the subject in general, the question of *who* the subject is asks for an identification of what we might call the *being* of the subject as a singular individual. As Jean-Luc Nancy in his contribution to the book observes, the question of the "who" of the subject has itself often been taken up as the question of the "what" of this "who" (see Nancy 1991, 7). It has been approached as the task of finding a "what"—the substance of the subject, the subject as substance—that lies underneath the "who" and that causes this "who" to be what it is. Nancy suggests that if we want to take the "who-question" seriously, we need to approach it in a different way, as the question of the "who" of the "who" (see Nancy 1991, 7). He explains: "But this is also a question: *who is who?* It is not "What is who?"—it is not a question of essence, but one of identity (as when one asks before a photograph of a group of people whose names you know but not the faces: "Who is who?"—is this one Kant, is that one Heidegger, and this other one beside him?" (Nancy, 1991, 7).

Nancy argues that this is a question of *presence*—"Who is *there*? Who is present there?" It is, however, "the presence of the existent: it is not an essence." This is why he further argues that we should not focus on the *presence* of the subject as such but rather on the *coming into presence* of the subject. Presence, after all, "*takes place,* that is to say it *comes into* presence" (Nancy 1991, 7). "There where there was nothing (and not even a 'there')," Nancy writes, "something, some *one* comes." *One* "because it 'comes,' not because of its substantial unity: the she, he, or it that comes can be one and unique in its coming but multiple and repeated 'in itself'" (Nancy 1991, 7). To ask the question of human subjectivity in this way, as a question about where the subject as a unique singular being—as some*one*—comes into presence, allows us to get away from the determination of the human subject as a substance or essence. It allows us to focus on the uniqueness and singularity of the event of *coming into presence* without having to explain "what" was there before "it" came into presence. Where, then, does the subject come into presence? And how does it come into presence as a unique, singular being? To develop an answer to these questions I now turn to a discussion of four different conceptions of space.

The Virtual Reality of Objective Space

The simple question of where the subject is has a long history in Western thought. It is perhaps not without significance that the first question God posed to man (Adam) is precisely a question of location: "Where are you?" (Genesis 3:9). In her essay "You Are Here: Information Drift" Laura Kurgan reveals that a definitive answer to the question "Where am I?"—"which some claim has troubled us from our origin" (Kurgan 1994, 17)—has finally been found. The answer is the Global Positioning System (GPS), a network of twenty-four satellites and five ground stations designed to provide anyone carrying a portable receiver with a highly specific determination of his or her location, anywhere, anytime, and in any weather. GPS promises that people and their vehicles will never get lost, that a world of stationary objects, from telephone poles to wetlands and private homes, will be fixed once and for all, and that missiles and bombs will land exactly where they ought to (Kurgan 1994, 18). As Paul Virilio makes clear, GPS "allows a rigorous orchestration of operations, but above all a perfect and automatic adequation between the positioning and the localization of weapons and war materials engaged in a conflict whose worldwide scope necessitates guidance, a flawless inertial navigation, in order to avoid provoking a chain of catastrophes whose impact on public opinion would be politically unsupportable" (Virilio, *L'écran désert* [*Desert Screen*], quoted in Kurgan 1994, 23).

It is not too difficult to see that the objectification of space brought about by the GPS is far from the definitive answer to the question of the location of the subject, the question of where the subject is. One problem is that GPS only identifies where someone is in relation to the system of satellites and ground stations. This means that for GPS to be able to provide effective orientation it first needs to re-identify the "real" world in terms of its own coordinates. If this is so—and Kurgan does argue persuasively that GPS does in fact replace the question "Where am I?" by the question "Which pixel am I standing on?" (see Kurgan 1994, 42)—then it shows that GPS does not so much offer an answer to the question "Where am I?" on the *earth* as to the question "Where am I?" on the *map*. GPS only offers a solution to the question of location in terms of one's position within a system, but to do this it needs to translate the "real" world into the world of GPS, thereby making the real world a virtual reality. GPS thus shows the problem with the idea of objective or absolute space and also shows that it cannot deliver on its promise to provide the final answer to the question "Where am I?"

The Space of Architecture: Disjunctive Space

It is often assumed that architecture provides a paradigm case for the idea of space. In the traditional conception of architecture space is *functional* space, its most basic function being the provision of shelter. According to Peter Eisenman, the relationship between function and form has been a defining characteristic of architecture from the Renaissance up to the twentieth century. As a result of the industrialization, function became increasingly more important than form, resulting, in the twentieth century, in the "oversimplified form-follows-function formula" (Eisenman 1976). According to Eisenman architecture has never really left the functionalist path. It has never become "modern" in the sense in which Eisenman defines modern, namely, as a "displacement of man away from the center of his world" (see Eisenman 1976). If architecture has never been modern, so Eisenman argues, then it follows that it can never be(come) postmodern either. It can, however, become *postfunctional*.

An example of such a postfunctional conception of architecture can be found in the work of architect/architectural theorist Bernard Tschumi. Tschumi challenges the traditional notion of architecture as an art of "pinning things down," of "fixing things" (Tschumi 1994a, 10). He challenges the notion of architectural space as "a given, a thing, that can be alternately served or serviced through specific programs" (Tschumi 1994a, 10). He challenges, in short, the functionalist conception of architecture, which rests upon the model of efficiency, that is, of the "seamless coincidence between space and its use," where "the building, our old machine, must 'work,' answering to its designated use" (Tschumi 1994a, 12).

Contrary to the conception of architecture as the formation of functional space—where the very organization of space through architecture is thought to prescribe the use of it so that any action exceeding this prescription can only be understood as misuse or disturbance—Tschumi advocates a definition of architecture "as the pleasurable and sometimes violent confrontation of spaces and activities" (Tschumi 1994b, 4). He advocates a definition of architecture as "simultaneously space and event" (Tschumi 1994b, 22). Instead of understanding the noncoincidence between space and its use as a failure, Tschumi argues that architecture's strength lies precisely in this "point of noncoincidence, of disjunction, of failure ... between the (supposed) cause-and-effect relations of ... use and space" (Tschumi 1994a, 11). Architecture and events "constantly transgress each other's rules," and it is this mutual transgression—disjunction—that should be our focus in understanding architecture. "A theory of architecture," he concludes, "is a theory of order threatened by the very use it permits. And vice versa." (Tschumi 1994b, 132).

Tschumi thus argues that the idea of architecture as the formation of functional space only tells half the story. He suggests that we should instead simultaneously understand architecture as space and event. This means that the disjunction of functional space, the noncoincidence of cause-and-effect relations, is the constitutive element of architecture, it is that which makes architecture actually possible. He even goes as far as to claim that "there is no space without event" (Tschumi 1994b, 139; see also Tschumi 1981). Space, we might say, only exists *by grace of the happening of events.* And events are by definition those happenings that can neither be foreseen nor controlled by the architectural program, but that "cross" the program and yet are also enabled by it.

Tschumi's conception of space—to which I will refer as *disjunctive space*—thus provides us with an understanding of space that is neither objectivistic nor phenomenological. The latter point is as important as the former, because although Tschumi's understanding of architectural space aims to give a central role to the active contribution of the subject, he does not reduce his conception of architectural space to the subject's individual, phenomenal *experience* of space. Architectural space is to be found—and we could also say: only exists, only comes into presence—in the disjunction of space and event. Tschumi therefore neither assumes the existence of "pure" space before the entering of a subject, nor does he assume the existence of a "pure" subject before its entering into space. Disjunctive space is a space of a constant mutual transgression, of an order constantly and necessarily threatened by the very use it permits. And it is in the very *moment* of disjunction that the subject, the user *and* abuser of space, comes into presence.

Tschumi's articulation of architectural space as disjunctive space is a helpful first step in developing an answer to the question of how the subject as a singular being comes into presence, in that he shows that the location or space where the subject comes into presence is not simply an environment or context "outside" of the subject, but that this space is in a complex, disjunctive—and, as I will discuss in more detail in Chapter 4, deconstructive—way tied up with the coming into presence of the subject, just as the subject itself is tied up in an equally complex way with the coming into presence of space. What is lacking in Tschumi's account, however, is an awareness of the social dimension of the space in which the subject comes into presence. For this I need to add another "layer" to my argument by exploring the idea of intersubjective space.

The Space of the Other: Intersubjective Space

The notion of intersubjective space is not meant to be a return to the very position I seek to overcome, that is, the humanistic reading of intersubjectivity. It rather is a way to stress that the coming into presence of the subject as a singular being, as some *one*, can only take place in what we might loosely refer to as a social situation. The point I wish to highlight in this section is that the question of who someone is cannot be resolved through introspection but needs an encounter with others. One way to understand what this entails is through Hannah Arendt's idea of *action*—an idea to which I will return in later chapters in more detail.

In her book *The Human Condition* (Arendt 1977b), Arendt makes a distinction among three fundamental human activities: labor, work, and action. While *labor* is the human activity "which corresponds to the biological process of the human body," and *work* is the activity that corresponds to the "unnaturalness of human existence" in that it provides an "artificial world of things, distinctly different from all natural surroundings," *action* is "the only activity that goes on directly between men [*sic*] without the intermediary of things or matter" (Arendt 1977b, 7).

To act, in its most general sense, means first of all to take initiative, that is, to begin. Action is therefore closely connected with the human condition of *natality*. "The new beginning inherent in birth can make itself felt in the world only because the newcomer possesses the capacity of beginning something anew, that is, of acting" (Arendt 1977b, 9). Arendt argues that if human beings were "endlessly reproducible repetitions of the same model, whose nature or essence was the same for all and as predictable as the nature or essence of any other thing," action would be an "unnecessary luxury" and a "capricious interference with general laws of behavior" (Arendt 1977b, 8). But Arendt stresses that human beings are *not* "endlessly reproducible repetitions of the same model." As she puts it, "we are all the same, that is, human, in such a way that nobody is ever the same as anyone else who ever lived, lives, or will live" (Arendt 1977b, 8). And it is through action that we disclose our "distinct uniqueness," that we "reveal actively [our] unique personal identities" (Arendt 1977b, 179).

The crucial thing about this disclosure is that it is *not* the revelation of some preexisting identity. Arendt stresses that nobody knows whom he reveals when he discloses himself in word and deed. This only becomes clear—both for the other and for the self—in action (see Arendt 1977b, 180). The crucial thing about action is, however, that we act upon beings "who are capable of their own actions" (Arendt 1977b, 190). Just as we strive to bring our beginnings into the world, others strive to bring their beginnings into the world as well. And it is only when our beginnings are taken up by others—others who are capable of their own actions—that we come into the world. This means that the agent that is disclosed in the act should not be understood as an "author" or "producer" but as a *subject* in the twofold sense of the word, namely, as one who began an action and as the one who suffers from its consequences (see Arendt 1977b, 184). But this "suffering" is a necessary suffering; it is the condition under which our beginnings can come into the world. Because human beings disclose themselves in action and because action acts upon beings who are capable of their own actions, the domain of action is "boundless" and "inherently unpredictable" (Arendt 1977b, 190–191). This is why action, the disclosure of the agent in a realm that only exists in between human beings, always entails a risk.

Arendt's idea of action clearly shows that the question of the "who" of the subject is a question that can only be answered by focusing on the ways in which individuals bring their beginnings into the world, that is, on the ways in which individuals come into presence. To this she adds that we only come into presence in those situations where we act upon beings who are capable of their own actions. To come into presence—and this is a crucial step in my argument—thus implies coming into a world populated by other beginners, a world of plurality and difference. To act is therefore more than simply to insert oneself into the world and forcing one's beginnings upon others (which, in Arendt's vocabulary, would be an example of work, not of action). The very point of her idea of action is that we can only act if *at the very same time* others can act as well, that is, if others are also able to bring their beginnings into the world. This is the reason why she emphasizes that "plurality is the condition of human action" (Arendt 1977b, 8). Arendt's notion of action thus displays recognition of the complexity of the subject's coming into presence that is similar to Tschumi's understanding of architectural space as disjunctive space. Coming into presence is not simply a process of presenting oneself to the world. It is about beginning in a world full of other beginners in such a way that the opportunities for others to begin are not obstructed. Coming into presence is, therefore, a presentation to others who are not like us. It is a presentation to, as Nancy puts it, a community "without the essence of a community" (Nancy 1991, 8), a community, as I will discuss in more detail in the next chapter, of those who have nothing in common. But what exactly is it that makes us unique in our coming into presence? How do we come into the world as a unique, singular being? To find an answer to this question I now turn to the work of Emmanuel Levinas.

The Space of Responsibility: Ethical Space

Levinas articulates an insight that comes quite close to the central idea of the notion of intersubjective space, namely, that our primordial being-in-the-world is a being-in-the-world-with-others. Levinas takes his point of departure in a critique of the common gesture of Western philosophy in which the *ego cogito,* or consciousness, is considered to come first, and in which the primary relationship of the ego with the world and with other beings is conceived as a knowledge-relationship. Levinas, however, wants to challenge the "wisdom of the Western tradition" in which it is assumed that "human individuals ... are human through consciousness" (Levinas 1998b, 190). He wants to challenge the idea "that subject and consciousness are equivalent concepts" (Levinas, 1989a, 92). To do so, he argues that the subject is engaged in a relationship that is "older than the ego, prior to principles" (Levinas, 1989a, 107). This relationship is neither a knowledge relationship—as there is not yet an ego or consciousness that can know—nor an act. Levinas characterizes it as an *ethical* relationship, a relationship of infinite responsibility for the other (see Levinas, 1989b).

Levinas stresses that this responsibility for the other is not a responsibility that we can either choose to take upon us or choose to neglect, since this would only be possible if we were an ego or consciousness *before* we were inscribed in this relationship. In this sense it is "a *responsibility that is justified by no prior commitment*" (Levinas 1989a, 92; emphasis in original). Levinas describes this responsibility as "an obligation, anachronously prior to any commitment," and as an "anteriority" that is "older than the a priori" (Levinas 1989a, 90), "older than the time of consciousness that is accessible in memory" (Levinas 1989a, 96). He also refers to this relation of responsibility as "an-archical" (Levinas 1989a, 92). By this he wishes to emphasize that it is a relationship with a singular other *without* "the mediation of any principle" (Levinas 1989a, 92). He calls it a "passion" and argues that this passion is absolute in that it takes hold "without any a priori" (Levinas 1989a, 92). He explains, "The consciousness is affected, then, before forming an image of what is coming to it, affected in spite of itself" (Levinas 1989a, 92). Levinas calls this relationship *obsession,* and he summarizes his point of view in the simple—though disturbing—phrase that "a subject is a hostage," obsessed with responsibilities "which did not arise in decisions taken by a subject" (Levinas 1989a, 101).

While Levinas is therefore in agreement with Arendt's contention that our primordial being is a being-with-others—we are with others before we are with ourselves; we are for the other before we are a oneself—he introduces a refinement or, better, a radicalization in stressing that this being-with-others is an *ethical* being-with-others, a being-with-others that is characterized by a primordial responsibility. In this respect we might say that the space where the subject comes into presence is an ethical space. It cannot be stressed enough, however, that Levinas is not talking about ethics in the traditional sense, that is, ethical behavior as being based upon a decision of the ego. "The ego is not just a being endowed with certain qualities called moral which it would bear as a substance bears attributes, or which it would take on as accidents in its becoming" (Levinas 1989a, 106).

It is not as if we can choose to be concerned for the other or not, for this question only has meaning "if one has already supposed that the ego is concerned only with itself" (Levinas 1989a, 107). It is precisely this assumption that Levinas denies. The subject is *not* something that is issued from one's own initiative (see Levinas 1989a, 95). It is not "an abstract point" or "the center of a rotation." It rather is "a point already identified from the outside" (Levinas 1989a, 96). It is "an assignation to answer without evasions, which assigns the self to be a self" (Levinas 1989a, 96).

We are "called" to be a self, so we could say, by the other. What makes us unique in this, is that the call is not a call to a human being in general; it is *me* who is called by the other. As Levinas explains, the oneself is the "not-being-able-to-slip-away-from an assignation," an assignation that does not aim at any generality, for it is "I and no one else" who is hostage (Levinas 1989a, 116). It is "a privilege or an unjustifiable election that chooses me and not the ego" (Levinas 1989a, 116). The oneself, therefore, "does not coincide with the identifying of truth, is not statable in terms of consciousness, discourse and intentionality" (Levinas 1989a, 96). The oneself is a singularity "prior to the distinction between the particular and the universal" and therefore "unsayable and unjustifiable" (Levinas 1989a, 97). In this sense, Levinas concludes, the oneself is *not* a being, because as a being it would still be a thing (see Levinas 1989a, 117). The oneself is "beyond the normal play of action and passion in which the identity of a being is maintained, in which it *is*" (Levinas 1989a, 104). While Levinas would therefore agree that the subject comes into presence in an intersubjective space, he takes this idea one step further by arguing that the subject as a unique and singular "being," as a "oneself," comes into presence because it finds itself in a situation where it cannot be replaced by anyone else. As Adrian Peperzak explains, "I am a hostage to the other and nobody can replace me in this service," and it is precisely this situation "which constitutes me as this unique individual" (Peperzak 1991, 62). My subjectivity is a subjection to the other, which means, in the shortest formula, that for Levinas "the subject is subject" (Critchley 1999, 63).

Conclusion

In this chapter I have explored how we might approach the question of the subject after the so-called death of the subject. I have shown that what is at stake in claims about the death of the subject and the end of man is *not* the erasure of the human subject as such. What is at stake is a critique of humanism, a critique of the idea that it is possible to define the essence of what it is to be human. With Foucault I have suggested that in order to overcome humanism, we should not seek for a new truth about the human subject but rather should envisage a new approach to the question of subjectivity. I have suggested that rather than looking for the substance or essence of the human being, we should ask the question *where* the human being as a unique individual comes *into presence.* My discussion of objective space has shown that no one—no *one*—comes into presence when the space of coming into presence can only relegate the subject to a certain fixed position, to a point on the map. As the idea of disjunctive space suggests, the coming-into-presence of unique, singular beings is not something that can be controlled by the space but is necessarily something that "interrupts" the program. This interruption should not be seen as a disturbance, as something that threatens the purity of space, but should be taken as a sign of some coming into presence. The discussion of intersubjective space shows that coming into presence is not something that one can do by oneself. One can bring one's beginning into the world, but one needs a world—a world made up of other "beginners"—in order to come into this world. One needs others who take up one's beginnings, always in new and unpredictable ways, in order to come into the world. This means that the social space, the space of intersubjectivity, is not a mirror in which we can finally see and find our true selves. The space of intersubjectivity, so we might say, is a "troubling" space, but this is a necessary troubling, a troubling that only makes our coming into the world possible. The discussion of ethical space suggests that long before we are a doer, a knower, an ego who can *take* responsibility, we are already identified, we are already positioned from the outside by a responsibility that is older than the ego. What makes me unique in this assignation, what singularizes me, what "makes" me into a unique, singular being, is not my identity, is not a set of attributes that only belongs to me, but is the fact that *I* am responsible and that *I* cannot slip away from this assignation. Interestingly enough, the discussion on ethical space suggests that the first question about the subject is not the question "Where am I?" but the question "Where are you?" The latter is the question that singularizes us, and it is this question that, in a very fundamental sense, can be understood as an educational question. It is the question that calls us into presence; or to be more precise, it is the question that calls *me*, as a singular being, as some *one*, into the world. This world, as I have emphasized throughout this chapter, is by necessity a world of plurality and difference; it is a world of otherness. I now turn to the question of how we might understand this world.

3

The Community of Those Who Have Nothing in Common

Education and the Language of Responsibility

What is, or what constitutes a community? In his book *The Community of Those Who Have Nothing in Common*, Alphonso Lingis observes that "community" is usually conceived as constituted by a number of individuals having something in common—a common language, a common conceptual framework—and building something in common: a nation, a polis, an institution (Lingis 1994, ix). A special instance of this kind of community is what Lingis calls the *rational community*. The rational community is not simply constituted by a common stock of observations, maxims for action, and common beliefs, but produces and is produced by a common discourse in a much stronger sense (Lingis 1994, 109). In the rational community "the insights of individuals are formulated in universal categories, such that they are detached from the here-now index of the one who first formulated them.... The common discourse is...a rational system in which, ideally, everything that is said implicates the laws and theories of rational discourse" (Lingis 1994, 110).

Membership of the rational community enables people to speak as "rational agents," that is, as representatives "of the common discourse" (Lingis 1994, 110). When we speak as a representative of the rational community, we are engaged in what Lingis calls "serious speech" (Lingis 1994, 112) "The seriousness in it is the weight of the rational imperative that determines what is to be said" (Lingis 1994, 112). What matters in serious speech, therefore, is *what* is said. We expect from doctors, veterinarians, or electricians that they speak according to the rules and principles of the rational discourse of the community of which they are a representative.

This implies, however, that the way in which things are said—"[t]he vocalization of what has to be said in this particular voice, by this particular speaker" (Lingis 1994, 112)—is *inessential.* "[T]he very saying is inessential, since what has to be said exists in the literature in the public libraries, or if not, is implicated already in the governing categories, theories, and methods of rational discourse" (Lingis 1994, 112). In the rational community we are therefore *interchangeable.* It does not really matter who says something, as long as what is said "makes sense." The rational community thus affords individuals a way into communication, but it is a very specific way. It is the way "by which one depersonalizes one's visions and insights, formulates them in terms of the common rational discourse, and speaks as a representative, a spokesperson, equivalent and interchangeable with others, of what has to be said" (Lingis 1994, 116).

It will not be too difficult to recognize the role of education—the role of schools and other educational institutions—in the constitution and reproduction of rational communities. Many people might well be inclined to argue that this is the main and perhaps even the only task of schools and the one and only reason for having schools in the first place. When we look at education from this perspective, we can see that schools do not simply provide students with a voice, they do not simply teach their students to speak. Schools provide students with a very specific voice, namely, with the voice of the rational communities it represents through the curriculum. In giving students such a voice, schools not only legitimize certain ways of speaking. At the very same time they delegitimize other ways of speaking. (This, as sociologists of education have shown us, explains why some students have to unlearn much more than others in order to succeed in the educational system.)

Modern Society: The Modern Community

Lingis depicts the rational community primarily in epistemological terms. For him the rational community is mainly an extension of what rational knowledge is, or of what certain groups hold rational knowledge to be (see, for example, Bloor 1976; Barnes 1977; Apple 1979). If we look at the idea of the rational community from a more sociological perspective, it could be argued that this community bears many if not all of the characteristics of what Zygmunt Bauman sees as being typical of modern society (which I put in the singular, because ultimately there can only be one rational society; see below).

Bauman describes modern society as a state of *order*. He argues that the modern "project" was meant to free individuals from "inherited identity" so as to give them "the benefit of an absolute beginning, set them free to choose the kind of life they wish to live and to monitor and manage its living in the framework of legal rules spelled out by the sole legitimate powers" (Bauman 1995, 203). The modern state wanted to free individuals from their premodern situatedness. The only way of doing this was by elevating individuals to something which itself was *beyond all tradition*. This not only meant that the state needed to engage in a systematic "discrediting, disavowing and uprooting of the intermediary powers of communities and traditions" (Bauman 1995, 203). It also meant that the state had to be guided by one singular, post-traditional vision to establish the post-traditional order.

Again, it might not be too difficult to recognize the role of modern education in this endeavor, because modern education has precisely been understood as the attempt to take children and students "beyond the present and the particular" (Bailey 1984) of their rooted identity, into the orderly, rational realm of modern society. Indeed, the ideal of modern education, as I have shown in the previous chapters, is to "release" children and students from their local, historical, and cultural situations and bring them into contact with a general, rational point of view (see Biesta 2002b).

What is important about Bauman's depiction of modern society is not only that it gives us a more empirical account of what a rational community might look like and suggests that modern society can ultimately be understood as a (the) rational community. He is also able to show how this community, the rational community of modern society, carried with it a very specific approach to what is outside of and other than itself, that is, the *stranger*. Strangers, according to Bauman, are those "who do not fit the cognitive, moral, or aesthetic map of the world" (Bauman 1995, 200). Bauman argues that all communities produce their own strangers. He emphasizes, however, that since modern society was based upon *one*, post-traditional vision, it could give no place to the strangers it produced (and perhaps we should repeat this in the present tense). The "progressive universalization of the human condition" (Bauman 1995, 202), which Bauman sees as *the* defining characteristic of modern society and modernity more generally, therefore dealt with the strangers it produced in two different, though related ways. The first strategy was one of assimilation, a strategy that Bauman characterizes as *anthropophagic* (which literally means man-eating): "annihilating the strangers by *devouring* them and then metabolically transforming them into a tissue indistinguishable from one's own" (Bauman 1995, 201). The other strategy was *anthropoemic*: "*vomiting* the strangers, banishing them from the limits of the orderly world and barring them from all communication with those inside" (Bauman 1995, 201). This is the strategy of *exclusion*, a strategy that ultimately resulted in the physical destruction of strangers (and perhaps we should repeat this in the present tense as well). The only option that was not considered was the idea of a *permanent coexistence* with the stranger. "The pragmatics of living with strangers," Bauman concludes, "did not need to be faced point blank as a serious project" (Bauman 1995, 202).

I wish to emphasize that the foregoing—and what follows—is not meant to suggest that all otherness or strangeness is simply good and simply has to be valued and respected because it is other and strange. There are real and very difficult questions to ask about, for example, the limits of toleration—one question being who has to tolerate who? The most important lesson to learn from the foregoing discussion concerns the way in which Bauman helps us to understand how the stranger is produced as a result of a specific construction of what is own, proper, familiar, rational. It is not to imply that everything that is other is categorically good. It is first and foremost to see that what counts as strange depends on what counts as familiar. The stranger, in other words, is never a natural category.

The Postmodern Stranger

If we combine Lingis's articulation of the rational community with Bauman's depiction of modern society, we can see that from the point of view of this community—that is, for those who are *inside* the community—those with whom we have nothing in common, the strangers, appear as a problem, as something that needs to be overcome, either by making the stranger similar to us or by making the stranger, or the strangeness of the stranger, invisible. It should not be forgotten, however, that the conclusion that strangers are a problem only follows, if we assume that the rational community is the only feasible, the only possible community, that it is, in more normative terms "the best of all possible worlds." Some people might argue that this is indeed the case, and the reason they might give for this—an "educational" reason—is that it is only through becoming a member of the rational community that people acquire a voice, an ability to speak. While the defenders of the rational community might abhor the idea that the rational community can only exists if it destroys the stranger, they might well be in favor of a strong version of assimilation. (Perhaps they are unable to see that this always also implies annihilation. Perhaps they want to argue that this is the price to be paid for the "progressive universalization" of humankind and the human condition.)

Bauman's response to the foregoing line of thinking is partly empirical, in that he argues that our "postmodern" society has changed so much that it simply is no longer viable to assume that the stranger can be kept outside. The postmodern stranger, he writes, is "here to stay" (Bauman 1995, 213). In a rather optimistic tone Bauman even argues that postmodern society has become *heterophilic* (Bauman 1995, 213), in that our "postmodern times are marked by an almost universal agreement that difference is not merely unavoidable, but good, precious, and in need of protection and cultivation" (Bauman 1995, 214). He hastens to add, however, that this should not lead to a reinstatement of the premodern plurality of "tribes," because in that case the essentialism of the modern project, the modern idea that ultimately there is only one right way to do and think, would only be replaced by another form of essentialism "where re-empowerment turns into a new disempowerment and emancipation into a new oppression" (Bauman 1995, 215).

Bauman sees a "genuine emancipatory chance" in postmodernity, "the chance of laying down arms, suspending border skirmishes waged to keep the stranger away, taking apart the daily erected mini-Berlin walls meant to keep distance and to separate" (Bauman 1995, 216). But this chance does *not* lie "in the celebration of born-again ethnicity and in genuine or invented tribal tradition" (Bauman 1995, 216). It doesn't lie in a return to forms of "strong community" such as the rational community, but rather "in bringing to its conclusion the 'disembedding' work of modernity, through laying bare the intricate process of subject self-formation, through revealing the conditions of individual freedom which … constitute the hard core of citizenship" (Bauman 1995, 216).

What Bauman is arguing for here, is that the genuine emancipatory chance of postmodernism is not to be found in a "new tribalism" in which we simply affirm our own, tribal identities. Instead, it needs to be connected to the question of what it means to be a subject, which for Bauman has to do with freedom and citizenship. The latter link—which Bauman has explored in much more detail in his *Postmodern Ethics* (Bauman 1993; see Biesta 2004a)—suggests that subjectivity, being a subject, is not something that has to do with the tribe we belong to (it is, in other words, not about our identity), but that it has to do with acting in a public space, the space where we are with others—or, in Bauman's terms, with *strangers*. He writes: "The chance of human togetherness depends on the rights of the stranger and not on the answer to the question who is entitled—the state or the tribe—to decide who the strangers are" (Bauman 1995, 216).

For Bauman, the emancipatory possibilities of postmodernity are thus to be found in our "membership" of a different community, a community in which we are all in a sense strangers for each other. This is the community to which Lingis refers as the community of those who have nothing in common.

The Community of Those Who Have Nothing in Common

Bauman's approach raises several questions. On a general level there is the question of how we should understand this "community without community" (Derrida 1997). On a more specific level there is the question of voice: What kind of voice, what kind of speech, and what kind of speaking are possible outside the confines of the rational community? And there is the question about what education can do or has to do in this constellation. To find an answer to the first two questions, we need to go back to Lingis.

We have seen that the rational community is constituted by a common language and a common logic. It gives us a voice, but only a representative voice. The rational community enables us to speak, but only in the language and logic of that community. Although it does matter *what* we say, it does not matter *who* is saying it, because in the rational community we are interchangeable. But what, then, does it mean to speak "outside" of the rational community? What voice can we use if we want to speak with the stranger, with the one with whom we don't share a common language?

Lingis examines two limit cases of communication to find an answer to this question. One case concerns the situation where we are with someone who is dying. What can one say in such a situation? Anything one tries to say sounds in a sense vacuous and absurd. But the point of speaking in such a situation, Lingis argues, is not about *what* you say. That almost doesn't matter—although we know all too well that we do not want to say the wrong thing. What matters most, what matters only is *that* you say something. The problem here is not simply that you do not have the skills in speaking or that you cannot come up with the right things to say because you have no experiences in this kind of situation. The problem is "that language itself does not have the powers" (Lingis 1994, 108).

There are two ways in which this situation is different from the way in which the rational community enables us to speak and gives us a voice. The first difference is that in this situation it almost no longer matters *what* you say but is of crucial importance *that* you say something, that you speak. This further implies that the voice with which you speak to the one with whom you have nothing in common is not a borrowed or representative voice, but has to be your *own* voice—and no one else's.

The other limit case Lingis discusses is the one where we are not at the end of language but at its beginning: the situation where parents and children communicate without being able to rely on the language, logic, and voice of the rational community, simply because the first communication comes *before* this community. This again is a situation in which the parent cannot speak to the child with the borrowed, representative voice of the rational community. What is required in this situation is that the parent responds and takes responsibility for the child in a unique, unprecedented and always new way. Lingis depicts this encounter as follows:

> It is the last warm day of the autumn; the mother has to go to the park with her child. She forgets all the letters she has to write and the conference she has to prepare for this weekend; she forgets all her friends. She is totally absorbed in her task. She is seated at the pool, and a rainbow gleams across the fountain in the late-autumn sun. She is pointing to the rainbow in the pool. Her eyes are open wide and gleaming, jubilation trembling the coaxing lines of her mouth. She has to lead his eyes to it. This day. His eyes are too young to be able to see the rainbow in the sky. Next year it will be too late; he will be in kindergarten, with eyes already jaded by the electronic rainbows on television screens; he will have to look at books with pictures associated with the letters of the alphabet. She has to fix the focus of his eyes and teach them to see it. She has to teach him the word: rainbow. Rainbow in the fountain. He has to learn the word and the wonder. She is wholly concentrated with the difficulty and the urgency of the task. She watches with anxiety and jubilation as the wonder fills his eyes, his eyes becoming wet with laughter, until she sees the rainbow in them. (Lingis 1994, 116–117)

Who, therefore, is speaking in these limit situations in which we cannot fall back upon the representative voice of the rational community? Lingis writes: "What is it that speaks in these terminal and inaugural situations? Not the ego as a rational mind, as a representative of universal reason that possesses the a priori categories and the a priori forms of the rational organization of sensory impressions. What speaks is someone in his or her materiality as an earthling" (Lingis 1994, 117).

This implies, that when I speak with the voice of the rational community, it is not really *me* who is speaking. My voice is simply the interchangeable voice of the rational community. But when I speak to the stranger, when I expose myself to the stranger, when I want to speak in the community of those who have nothing in common, then I have to find my own voice, then it is *me* who has to speak—and no one else can do this for me. It is, to put it differently, this very way of speaking that constitutes me as a unique individual—as *me*, and no one else.

The Language of Responsibility

Although we can now see who it is that has to speak in the encounter with the stranger, we need to say a bit more about the language that we can use in this encounter. What is it that we can say when we speak for ourselves, outside of the confines of the rational community? What language can we use? I want to suggest that the language that we use in such encounters should not be understood as language in the sense of a set of words or utterances. What matters is not the content of what we say, but what is *done*. And what is done, what needs to be done, and what only I can do, is to *respond* to the stranger, to be *responsive* and *responsible* to what the stranger asks from me. To quote Lingis once more:

> The other turns to me and speaks; he or she asks something of me. Her words, which I understand because they are the words of my own tongue, ask for information and indications.

They ask for a response that will be responsible, will give reasons for its reasons and will be a commitment to answer for what it answers. But they first greet me with an appeal for responsiveness. (Lingis 1994, 130–131)

The "language" with which we can speak with the stranger, the "language" that gives us our own, unique and singular voice is, in other words, the language of responsivity and responsibility. It does not matter what words we use—because there are, in a sense, no words. It only matters that we respond, that we take responsibility, that we take *our* responsibility.

This means, however, that the community of those who have nothing in common, the community of strangers, the community without community, is of an ethical nature. The community of those who have nothing in common is constituted by our response to the stranger, the one who asks, seeks—demands, as Levinas would say—*my* response, who seeks to hear *my* unique voice.

The only way in which we can speak with our own voice, is when we let go of our other voice. This means that the "other community" is a "community that demands that the one who has his own communal identity, who produces his own nature, expose [*sic*] himself to the one with whom he has nothing in common, the stranger"(Lingis 1994, 10). Lingis emphasizes that exposing oneself to the stranger, exposing oneself to "an imperative" (Lingis 1994, 11), is not something one does with one's rational intelligence. It is not, in other words, that our response is based on knowledge of the other. It is not that we first have to know what we will be responsible for and only then can decide to take up this responsibility. The language of responsibility is, in other words, not about calculation. It is in a very fundamental sense without ground, and it is in an equally fundamental sense unlimited. Derrida explains this insight as follows.

When the path is clear and given, when a certain knowledge opens up the way in advance, the decision is already made, it might as well be said that there is none to make; irresponsibly, and in good conscience, one simply applies or implements a program.... It makes of action the applied consequence, the simple application of a knowledge or know-how. It makes of ethics and politics a technology. No longer of the order of practical reason or decision, it begins to be irresponsible. (Derrida 1992, 45)

The Rational Community and the "Other" Community

One final point to make in this exploration of the idea of "community" is that the rational community and the "other" community should not be understood as two separate communities and also not as two options that we can choose from. There is no way to deny the importance of the rational community—or rational communi*ties*—since they make certain ways of speaking and doing possible. We should, of course, not forget that this speaking is only a representative speaking. And we also should not forget that each time a rational community is constituted, it draws a borderline, it creates at the very same time an inside and an outside. Lingis writes: "The community that produces something in common, that establishes truth and that now establishes a technological universe of simulacra, excludes the savages, the mystics, the psychotics—excludes their utterances and their bodies" (Lingis 1994, 13).

Lingis therefore concludes that the other community forms, comes into presence, in the *interruption* of the work and the enterprises of the rational community. The other community "recurs, ... troubles the rational community, as its double or its shadow" (Lingis 1994, 10). It lives "inside" the rational community as a constant possibility and comes into presence as soon as one responds to the other, to the otherness of the other, to what is strange in relation to the discourse and logic of the rational community. It comes into existence when one speaks in one's own voice, with the voice that is unique, singular, and unprecedented. The voice that has never been heard before.

The Community of Education

The foregoing exploration of the idea of "community" reveals that there are (at least) two different ways to understand what it might mean to be, to live with others. Both forms of community provide an "entry into communication" (Lingis 1994, 116), but it is precisely in the way in which the two communities enable us to speak that there is a crucial difference. There is not only a difference in that in the rational community it matters *what* is said, while in the other community it matters *who* is speaking. It is also that in the rational community our voice is a *representative voice*, while it is only in the other community that we speak in *our own*, unique and unprecedented way. This in turn means that it is only in and through our engagement with the other community, that is, in and through the way we expose ourselves to what is strange and other, that we come into the world as unique and singular beings—and not as instances of some more general "form" of what it is to be human.

In passing I have already mentioned a connection between the rational community and education, by arguing that the most visible function of schools seems to lie in their role of initiating children and students into the/a rational community. The two forms of community that I have distinguished in this chapter can also be connected to the two approaches to learning that I introduced in Chapter 1. I argued there that the most common—and presumably most influential—conception of learning sees learning in terms of *acquisition*: the acquisition of something external, such as knowledge, values, or skills, something that existed before the act of learning and that becomes the possession of the learner as a result of her learning. Although there are many different theories about this kind of learning, ranging from accounts of learning in terms of changes in the brain to accounts of learning as a thoroughly social endeavor, all such theories rely on the idea of learning as acquisition. The idea of learning as acquisition fits the rational community quite well. One can indeed argue that the only way in which individuals can become a member of the rational community is through the acquisition of the forms of knowledge, the logic, and the values that make up the/a rational community. And one can further argue that the educational systems in many countries are precisely based on this idea.

There is, however, another way to understand learning, one that does not think of learning as the acquisition of something that already exists, but instead sees learning as responding, as a response to a "question." If we look at learning in this way, we can say that someone has learned something *not* when she is able to copy and reproduce what already existed, but when she responds to what is unfamiliar, what is different, what challenges, irritates, or even disturbs. Here learning becomes a creation or an invention, a process of bringing something new into the world: one's own, unique response.

I am inclined to believe that the latter learning is educationally the most significant and important form, since it has to do with ways in which we come into presence as unique, singular beings. As educators we should neither deny nor forget that we live in a world of rational communities, that these communities are important for specific purposes, and that the main reason why we have schools, at least from a historical point of view, is in order to reproduce the world of rational communities. But we also shouldn't forget that this is not all that matters in life—and that it is perhaps even the case that what ultimately matters is not the reproduction of rational communities but the possibility for the other community to come and to stay into existence. If the other community would no longer be possible, then we could say that the world has come to an end, since if the world would only be a rational community, then it would no longer matter who would live in that world and who would not. We would, after all, all be interchangeable.

This is what makes the other community, the community of those who have nothing in common, so important for education—and one of the questions that needs to be asked is how much of the other community is actually possible in our schools. The problem with the other community, however, is that it cannot be brought into existence in any deliberate or technical way. The other community is *not* the result of work, it doesn't come into existence through the application of a technique or technology. In this respect the other community can never become a new educational tool or a new educational program. We cannot make or force our students to expose themselves to what is other and different and strange. The only thing we can do is to make sure that there are at least opportunities within education to meet and encounter what is different, strange, and other, and also that there are opportunities for our students to really respond, to find their own voice, their own way of speaking. We, as teachers and educators, should be aware that what disrupts the smooth operation of the rational community is not necessarily a disturbance of the educational process, but might well be the very point at which students begin to find their own, responsive and responsible voice.

Conclusion

In this chapter I have explored the notion of "community" in order to understand in more detail what it means to come into a world populated by others who are not like us. The central claim of this chapter is that our subjectivity, that which makes us into unique, singular beings, is of an ethical "nature." It is in and through the ways in which we respond to the other, to the otherness of the other, to what is strange and different to us—and to respond means to be responsive and take responsibility—that we come into the world as unique, singular beings.

Following Bauman we can say that this way of understanding our subjectivity neither reduces who we are to the communities, tribes, or clans that we are part of (our identity), nor elevates our subjectivity to some universal mode of rationality. The emancipatory potential of the approach explored in this book lies precisely in envisaging a third way of understanding subjectivity: beyond identity and universality. Against this background I have argued that we should think of education as being first and foremost concerned with the opportunities for human beings to come into the world, to find their own voice, to constitute themselves as unique, singular beings. The first concern for education, to put it differently, is about how children and students can learn to speak in their own voice. This is not to exclude or deny the role of education and schooling in the reproduction of the rational community, but it does raise the question of how much of the other community is possible within the educational system and also what it requires from education to make this possible—a question that I will address in the next chapter.

The categories that I have used in this chapter are not those of epistemology and metaphysics, but those of ethics and politics. I have argued that the origin of our subjectivity is not to be thought of in terms of our consciousness or rational mind (epistemology), and that it cannot be thought of as an essence, as something that we possess or that is our fundamental ground (metaphysics). What constitutes our subjectivity, what constitutes us in our subjectivity is the way in which we—you and I as singular beings—respond. We may want to call this our response-ability, as long as we are aware that this ability is not our ultimate (metaphysical) essence. There is, after all, no guarantee that people will respond, no mechanism that can make us respond. It only is a possibility. We might be vulnerable beings, but vulnerability never automatically translates into responsibility and responsive action.

Responsibility, as I have argued, is not about what we already know. Responsibility excludes and opposes calculation.

It is precisely for this reason that responsibility is related to the community of those who have nothing in common. It ultimately is this community that makes our "second birth," our coming into the world as unique, individual beings, possible. Like our first, physical birth, this is not necessarily a pleasant experience. It can be difficult and painful to come into the world, to take upon us the responsibility that is waiting for us, to expose ourselves to what is other and different. Yet this is what makes us unique and, in a certain sense, human.

4

How Difficult Should Education Be?

One of the remarkable things about Western education is the persistence of *technological expectations* about education and schooling. This can, for example, be seen in the pressure that governments of many countries put on the educational system to improve its performance, which more often than not means a requirement to deliver specific, predetermined outcomes. Such pressure is both exerted on the educational system as a whole, for example through national curricula or international monitoring of student performance and on individual schools, classrooms, and teachers, for example through the publication of school league tables and ever tighter systems of inspection and control.

The technological attitude toward education, the idea that education is a means or an instrument that can be used to bring about certain predetermined ends, has many different faces. Not only are there technological expectations about the transmission of knowledge and skills, but recent calls for character education, certain conceptions of citizenship education, or the idea that education can be used to counteract social disintegration are all examples of technological expectations about education in the area of values and norms. The technological attitude also isn't the exclusive privilege of right-wing politicians pursuing a conservative educational agenda. The leftist hope that society can be changed through education, that schools can build a "new social order" (Counts 1939), is based on a similar set of expectations about what education can achieve. Moreover, governments and policymakers are not the only actors in the public arena who are increasingly holding the educational system accountable for its performance. Many parents no longer see themselves in relation to the schools of their children as fellow educators, but have come to redefine their position as one of consumers of the educational commodities, which schools are supposed to deliver (see Biesta 2004a).

The main assumption behind the technological attitude is the idea that education is an instrument that can be put to work to bring about certain predetermined ends. On the "positive" side, this leads to the idea that the improvement of education is to be found in the development of better means—which leaves educational research mainly with the task of better educational techniques and strategies, instead of contributing to a critical discussion about the aims and ends of education. On the "negative" side, the technological view of education brings with it the view that in those cases in which education is *not* successful in achieving its aims, that is, where education is *difficult,* or where education even appears to be impossible, that such a result is a deviation from the normal course of events—which, in turn, suggests that these hindrances are seen as merely of a technical order so that, in principle, one day when we have found the right way to proceed, they can be overcome.

In this chapter I want to look at the difficulty of education from a different angle. I want to argue that an adequate understanding of the process of education requires that we think in a different order about what is normal and what is deviant, that is, that we should *not* think of the difficulty of education as a deviation, as a danger, a threat, or a disturbance that comes from the "outside." I will suggest that we should rather conceive of this difficulty as something that is proper, that belongs to education, as something that makes education possible in the first place. I want to argue, in other words, that our understanding of education should start from this very difficulty of education (see Donald 1992).

The approach that I will explore in this chapter might be characterized as a *deconstructive* understanding of education, in that I will attempt to understand the "logic" of the process of education in terms of the idea that the condition of possibility of education is at the same time its condition of impossibility (see Derrida 1988; Caputo 1997; Biesta 2001). This claim should be read extremely carefully. The deconstructive line of thought that I advance in this chapter is not an attempt to suggest that education is simply impossible—and therefore futile. It rather is an attempt to think differently about education and to show that what makes education difficult and sometimes even impossible, is precisely what makes education possible in the first place (see, for example, Vanderstraeten and Biesta 2001; Biesta 2004b). To "read" education deconstructively should help us to see that it is possible to understand education outside of the confines of a technological framework, outside of the confines of the technological attitude. This is particularly important in relation to a point made in Chapter 3, where I argued that the "other community," the community of those who have nothing in common, cannot be brought into existence in a deliberate or technical way and for that matter can never become a new educational technique. If it is the case that the "other community" is the community through which individuals can come into the world as unique, singular beings, it is of crucial importance that this community is not beyond educational reach, even if it cannot be brought about by applying a particular educational technique.

The approach that I will pursue in this chapter is, in a sense, oblique in that I will examine the difficulty of education through the lens of the difficulty of politics and the political. The main reason for this is that questions about the difficulty of human interaction have been discussed much more poignantly in the context of politics than they have been within education. The ideas that I will discuss in this chapter are, however, extremely relevant for education because with respect to the overarching issue of the difficulty of human interaction there is no fundamental difference—and perhaps not even a gradual difference—between the realm of politics and the realm of education. What is it, then, that makes human interaction difficult?

Politics and the Political Community

The difficulty of human interaction stems from the fact that, as Hannah Arendt has put it, "men, not Man, live on the earth and inhabit the world" (Arendt 1977b, 7). It stems, in other words, from the existence of plurality, diversity, and difference. One of the most fundamental questions for politics and political theory, therefore, is the question of how to respond to the fact of plurality. In her book *Political Theory and the Displacement of Politics,* Bonnie Honig argues that Western philosophy has generally developed two different strategies for answering this question (Honig 1993). She argues that most political theorists confine politics to the task of building consensus, maintaining agreements, and consolidating communities and identities. They assume that the success of politics lies in the elimination of dissonance, resistance, conflict, and struggle. They see it as the basic task of politics "to resolve institutional questions" and to "free modern subjects ... of political conflict and instability" (Honig 1993, 2)

Whereas these theorists—to which Honig refers as *virtue* theorists—believe that their favored principles and institutions fit and express the identities of subjects, *virtù* theorists, on the other hand, argue that no such fit is possible. They stress that every political settlement has its remainders and that resistances are actually engendered by every political settlement, "even by those that are relatively enabling or

empowering" (Honig 1993, 3) It is for the sake of these per-
petually generated remainders that *virtù* theorists seek to
secure the perpetuity of political contest. (The distinction between *virtue* theorists and *virtù* theorists does not correspond
to the distinction between liberals and communitarians. The
ingenuity of Honig's approach lies precisely in the fact that
she is able to show that liberals *and* communitarians can
be seen as proponents of the same political "style." Honig
therefore presents both Rawls and Sandel (and also Kant)
as *virtue* theorists. She discusses Nietzsche and Arendt as
representatives of the *virtù* approach.)

Honig's analysis reveals that there is a distinction between
those who see plurality as something that can and should
be overcome by politics (the *virtue* theorists) and those who
believe that plurality cannot be overcome by politics and
that it also should not be overcome (the *virtù* theorists). On
the surface *virtue* theorists seem to be correct. Politics, so one
could argue, exists for the very sake of establishing a social
order, given the existence of substantive differences. One
could question, of course, whether any social order can ever
be fully inclusive (as *virtue* theorists assume), or whether it
can only be established by an act of division and exclusion, in
which case there always and necessarily will be remainders.
This difference, however, seems more of a gradual than essential kind, although Honig rightly shows that those who
assume that a social order can be fully inclusive exhibit a
rather undemocratic insensitivity to the remainders of their
politics, even "as they depend on those remainders to stabi-
lize their orders" (Honig 1993, 4).

The question that interests me here, however, is not *whether*
politics has to deal with plurality or not—it simply has
to—but *how* politics should deal with plurality. In the light
of the latter question I see a more subtle difference between
virtue theories and *virtù* theories. What distinguishes *virtue*
theories from *virtù* theories is that the former conceive of
plurality and difference as a difficulty or a problem for which
politics has to provide the solution. *Virtue* theories, to be

more precise, conceive of plurality as a hindrance to social life, as a disturbance and a *weakness,* and they see politics as the cure for this weakness. The implicit assumption here is that social life is only possible if there is a sufficient degree of commonality or agreement between those living together. *Virtue* theorists therefore see it as the basic task for politics to install a political community, a community that has enough in common—which means, a community that is sufficiently depluralized—for social life to become possible.

The latter strategy can, for example, be found in some versions of liberal political theory. Liberalism, in the words of John Rawls, seeks to articulate an ideal of political order that can deal with the "fact of pluralism" in a non-oppressive way (see Rawls 1993, 192). Its aim is to find an answer to the question of how to organize coexistence among people with different conceptions of the good without giving prevalence to any of these conceptions. The two main components of its answer are the idea of the priority of the right over the good and the distinction between the private and the public sphere. The first principle entails the claim that individual rights cannot be sacrificed for the sake of the general good *and* that the principles of justice that specify these rights cannot be premised on any particular vision of the good. The aim, therefore, is to develop a fair framework within which individuals can choose their own values and ends, consistent with a similar liberty for others. The distinction between the private and the public sphere is made to indicate where the proliferation of conceptions of the good is allowed (in the private sphere) and where it is not (in the public sphere).

This shows that there is at least a tendency in liberal political philosophy to see plurality as something that poses a threat to social life. The solution that is proposed is the creation of a particular kind of political community, the "public sphere," which can be characterized as a depluralized community. In this way, as Chantal Mouffe has argued, liberalism tries to secure a consensus in the public realm by relegating all pluralism and dissent to the private domain.

All controversial issues are taken off the political agenda in order to create the conditions for a rational consensus (see Mouffe 1993, 140).

Although liberalism does address the issues of plurality, it is clear that it does so by removing as much plurality as possible from the public realm. It represents an attempt to develop a minimal shared political framework that allows for maximum expression of diversity outside of politics. Besides the more practical question of whether it is possible to make a clear distinction between what is private and what is public (notorious examples of the contrary are abortion and euthanasia), there is the more fundamental problem that liberalism—and this is a problem for all *virtue*-theories—appears to think of politics as something for like-minded people. Although liberalism tries to be as inclusive as possible in social life, it does so by excluding plurality from the realm of politics. The danger is that political participation becomes only open for those who already agree on the rules of the game.

My aim here is not to argue for or against liberalism, but to present the version of liberal political philosophy outlined previously, as an example of a particular conception of what constitutes a political community—a conception that sees plurality and difference as a hindrance, as something that needs to be overcome. Whether this is a viable conception of politics is, in a sense, an empirical question (although there are also complex theoretical issues at stake), although I do agree with Mouffe that a negation of the fact that every political order, including a liberal one, generates its own remainders, does not make these remainders disappear, but runs the risk of leading "to a bewilderment in the face of its manifestations and to impotence in dealing with them" (Mouffe 1993, 140).

Although it is important to ask to what extent *virtue*-theories offer a realistic program for political life, it is at least as important to raise the question as to whether *virtù* theories provide a viable alternative, that is, whether it is possible to think of the relationship between plurality and politics—and hence of the role of plurality in human interaction—in such a way that it is *not* seen as a weakness or a threat but rather as something that is central to it. One of the few philosophers who has explored this road is Hannah Arendt.

Hannah Arendt and the Difficulty of Politics

Hannah Arendt is unambiguously clear about the position of plurality in her understanding of politics. On the first page of the first chapter of *The Human Condition* she declares that plurality, the fact that "men, not Man, live on the earth and inhabit the world," is "*the* condition ... of all political life." Plurality is not only "the *conditio sine qua non*" of political life, that is, the condition without which political life would not exist. It is also "the *conditio per quam*" of political life, that is, the ultimate condition of political life, the condition through which political life exists (Arendt 1977b, 7).

Plurality is one of three conditions under which "life on earth has been given to man." These conditions (see below) correspond to three fundamental activities—labor, work, and action—which together comprise the *vita activa*. The *vita activa* is the life of *praxis* that Arendt wants to restore to its proper place from which it had been dispelled since the beginning of Western philosophy by the life of contemplation, the *vita contemplativa*.

Arendt describes *labor* as the activity that corresponds to the biological process of the human body. Labor stems from the necessity to maintain life and is focused exclusively on the maintenance of life. It does so in endless repetition—"one must eat in order to labor and must labor in order to eat" (Arendt 1977b, 143). The human condition of labor, therefore, is "life itself" (Arendt 1977b, 7). *Work,* on the other hand, is the activity that corresponds to the "unnaturalness" of human existence. *Work* provides an artificial world of things, distinctly different from all natural surroundings. It is concerned with *making* and for that reason it is "entirely determined by the categories of means and end," that is, with *instrumentality* (Arendt 1977b, 143). Since work is concerned with the fabrication of a world of objects that has durability and permanence, it also has "objectivity" (Arendt 1977b, 137). The human condition of work, therefore, is "worldliness" (Arendt 1977b, 7).

Whereas labor and work are concerned with the interaction of human beings with the material world, *action* is the activity "that goes directly between men," without "the intermediary of things or matter" (Arendt 1977b, 7). To act, in its most general sense, means to take an initiative, that is, to begin. Arendt argues that man is an *"initium,"* a "beginning and a beginner" (Arendt 1977a, 170). In this respect every act is a "miracle" in that it is "something which could not be expected" (Arendt 1977a, 169). Action is most closely related to one of the most general conditions of human existence: the condition of *natality*. Action as beginning corresponds to the fact of birth, because with each birth something "uniquely new" comes into the world. Action is the "actualization of the human condition of natality" (Arendt 1977b, 178).

The reason why action corresponds to the human condition of plurality lies in the fact that we always act upon beings "who are capable of their own actions" (Arendt 1977b, 190). If men were "endlessly reproducible repetitions of the same model" action would be "an unnecessary luxury, a capricious interference with the general laws of behavior" (Arendt 1977b, 8). But this is not the case. *Plurality* is the condition of human action because "we are all the same"—that is, we are all capable of beginning—"in such a way that nobody is ever the same as anyone else who ever lived, lives, or will live" (Arendt 1977b, 8).

On the "negative" side—I will return to the special character of this negativity below—the fact that we act upon beings who are capable of their own actions implies that the domain of action is boundless and inherently unpredictable (see Arendt 1977b, 190–191). Arendt writes that the exasperation with the "frustration of action" is almost as old as recorded history. It has, therefore, always been a great temptation to find a substitute for action "in the hope that the realm of human affairs may escape the haphazardness ... inherent in a plurality of agents" (Arendt 1977b, 220). The proposed solutions always amount to seeking shelter from action's calamities in an activity where "one man remains master of his doings from beginning to end" (Arendt 1977b, 220). This attempt to replace acting with making, that is, to conceive of politics in terms of *work* and hence of instrumentality, is manifest "in the whole body of argument against 'democracy,'" and will eventually turn into an argument against the essentials of politics itself (Arendt 1977b, 220).

The reason why Arendt argues that this is so stems from the fact that action is not a cosubjective process. It is not a process in which individuals *work* together and produce things. Arendt acknowledges that man's capacity to act, and especially to act in concert, is "extremely useful for purposes of self-defense or of pursuit of interest" (Arendt 1977b, 179). But "if nothing more would be at stake than to use action as a means to an end," it is obvious that the same end could be attained much more easily—for which reason she concludes that "action seems a not very efficient substitute for violence" (Arendt 1977b, 179). The point, however, is that there *is* more at stake—and here we touch upon the "positive" implication of the fact that we act upon beings who are capable of their own actions. (I will also return to the special character of this positivity below.)

Why, then, is action important? We have seen that for Arendt human plurality is the "paradoxical plurality" of *unique* beings: We are all the same in that nobody is ever the same as anyone else. Arendt's point is that it is only in action and *not* in labor or work—that our "unique distinctness" is revealed. "With word and deed," she writes, "we insert ourselves into the human world, and this insertion is like a second birth" (Arendt 1977b, 176). Action and speech are, therefore, the modes in which human beings appear or come into the world, and this is *by necessity* an appearance to others. Although the revelation of the agent in the act is in a very fundamental sense something that we do, it is in an evenly fundamental sense *not* something that we can refrain from. Action and speech retain their "agent-revealing capacity" even if their *content* is concerned with labor or work. Disclosure is, in this sense, *inevitable* (Arendt 1977b, 183).

As I have emphasized in Chapter 2, the event of disclosure is not the disclosure of some preexisting identity. Arendt stresses "that nobody knows whom he reveals when he discloses himself in deed or word" (Arendt 1977b, 180). This only becomes clear in the sphere of action. The agent that is disclosed in the act is therefore not an author or a producer, but a subject in the twofold sense of the word, namely, as one who began an action and as the one who suffers from its consequences (see Arendt 1977b, 184). And precisely here lies the inherent "risk of disclosure" (Arendt 1977b, 180).

Although the human condition of plurality in a sense always frustrates our action, Arendt stresses again and again that it is only because of the specific character of the "medium" of action that action alone is real (Arendt 1977b, 184). It indicates, therefore, something "that frustrates action in terms of its own purposes" (Arendt 1977b, 182). It is for this reason that the negative implications of the fact that we always act upon beings who are capable of their own actions are not simply or straightforwardly negative, just as the positive implications are not simply or straightforwardly positive. And it is precisely here that the deconstructive character of Arendt's understanding of politics—and of human interaction more generally—comes to the fore.

The Predicament of Action

The central idea of Arendt's position lies in the claim that human beings are beginnings and beginners. In the sphere of human interaction we therefore always act upon beings who are capable of their own actions. We always begin our beginnings, to put it differently, in a world populated by other beginners. This means, however, that in order to pursue our own beginnings we always have to rely on the actions of other beginners. Although, in a sense, this frustrates and disturbs the "purity" of our beginning, this "impossibility to remain unique masters of what [we] do" is at the very same time the condition—and the only condition—under which our beginnings can ever come into the world (see Arendt 1977b, 220). Action, as distinguished from fabrication, is never possible in isolation. Arendt even argues that "to be isolated is to be deprived of the capacity to act" (Arendt 1977b, 188).

Although the predicament of action played a central role in the Greek and Roman political context, Arendt argues that the distinction between the beginning of an act made by a single person and the achievement of an act "in which many join by 'bearing' or 'finishing' the enterprise" (Arendt 1977b, 189) has gradually disappeared from the way in which the Western tradition has understood action. The "dependence of the beginner upon others for help and the dependence of his followers upon him for an occasion to act themselves" (Arendt 1977b, 189) split into two altogether different functions: the function of giving commands and the function of executing them. Arendt claims that the greater part of political philosophy since Plato has tried to find theoretical foundations and practical ways to safeguard that a beginner can remain the complete master of what he has begun (see Arendt 1977b, 222). What was lost in this process was the insight that it is only with the help of others that the "ruler, beginner and leader" can really act, can really carry through "whatever he had started to do" (Arendt 1977a, 166).

The foregoing remarks can help us understand why the fact that the domain of action is "boundless" and inherently "unpredictable" is not straightforwardly negative. It is, after all, precisely this boundlessness and unpredictability that makes it possible for our beginnings to come into the world and thus become real. Arendt's understanding of action reveals that what makes our being with others *difficult* is at the very same time that which makes our being with others *possible*—that is to say, as long as we conceive of our being with others as being with *others*. There is, after all, always the option of enforcing our beginnings upon others, thereby denying and eradicating the otherness of the other. This is the point where action turns into making, that is, where the mode of activity becomes technological.

freedom, Action, and Plurality

Just as the negative implication of the boundlessness of action reveals a deconstructive "twist" in Arendt's thought, the positive implication of this boundlessness is not straightforward either. This becomes clear in Arendt's approach to the question of freedom. Arendt argues that freedom should not be understood as a phenomenon of the will, that is, as the freedom to do whatever we choose to do, but that we should rather conceive of it as the freedom "to call something into being which did not exist before" (Arendt 1977a, 151). The subtle difference between freedom as sovereignty and freedom as beginning has far-reaching consequences. The main implication is that freedom is not an "inner feeling" or a private experience, but that it is by necessity a public and hence a political phenomenon. "The *rasion d'etre* of politics is freedom," she argues, "and its field of experience is action" (Arendt 1977a, 146).

Arendt argues that this freedom—which "even those who praise tyranny must still take into account"—and which is the opposite of inner freedom, that is, of "the inward space into which men may escape from external coercion and *feel* free" (Arendt 1977a, 146), is the most original form of freedom. It seems safe to say "that man would know nothing of inner freedom if he had not first experienced a condition of being free as a worldly tangible reality" (Arendt 1977a, 148). According to Arendt we first become aware of freedom or its opposite in our intercourse with others and not in the intercourse with ourselves. The experience of inner freedom is therefore *derivative* in that it presupposes "a retreat from a world where freedom was denied" (Arendt 1977a, 146).

The problem with freedom as inner freedom is that it remains without outer manifestations. For that very reason it is "by definition politically irrelevant" (Arendt 1977a, 146). Arendt stresses again and again that freedom needs a "worldly space," a "public realm" to make its appearance (Arendt 1977a, 149) "To be sure," Arendt writes, "it may still dwell in men's hearts as desire or will or hope or yearning; but the human heart, as we all know, is a very dark place, and whatever goes on in its obscurity can hardly be called a demonstrable fact" (Arendt 1977a, 149). Contrary, therefore, to the idea that freedom only begins "where men have left the realm of political life inhabited by the many" (Arendt 1977a, 157), Arendt proposes a *political* understanding of freedom in which freedom is only real, where freedom only exists if it appears in a public space.

One of the main implications of the public character of freedom is that we can no longer think of freedom as something that individual beings possess. Freedom only exists *in action,* which means that men *are* free—as distinguished from their "possessing the gift of freedom"—as long as they act, "neither before nor after" (Arendt 1977a, 153, 157).

Since freedom only exists in the act, Arendt suggests that we might think of it in terms of the performing arts (as distinguished from the creative arts of making) (see Arendt 1977a, 153–154). There are two reasons for suggesting this connection. The first lies in the fact that, contrary to the creative arts of making, the accomplishments of performing arts lie in the performance itself and not in an end product that outlasts the activity that brought it into existence and becomes independent of it. The "quality" of the creative act is, in other words, not appreciated through its product but lies in the "virtuosity" (Arendt 1977a, 153) of the performance. Second, Arendt argues that performing artists need an audience to show their virtuosity "just as acting men need the presence of others before whom they can appear" (Arendt 1977a, 154). The difference here is, of course, not that the creative arts of making can do without an audience. The crucial issue is that the performing arts *depend* on others for the performance itself. Unlike a painting, a performance without an audience doesn't exist. Actors—in the double sense of the word—need—a "publicly organized space for their 'work'" (Arendt 1977a, 154).

Arendt's account of freedom thus reveals that freedom only exists in our being with others. Freedom only exists, to put it differently, "under the condition of nonsovereignty" (Arendt 1977a, 164). Arendt stresses that within the conceptual framework of traditional philosophy it is very difficult to understand how freedom and nonsovereignty can exist together. Yet under human conditions, which are determined by the fact of plurality, "freedom and sovereignty are so little identical that they cannot even exist simultaneously" (Arendt 1977a, 164). "If men wish to be free," Arendt summarizes, "it is precisely sovereignty they must renounce" (Arendt 1977a, 165). Again, therefore, we can say that what makes freedom difficult—the fact of plurality—is what makes freedom possible.

The Space Where Freedom Can Appear

The foregoing overview reveals that Arendt consistently tries to understand human interaction in general, and political life in particular, from the point of view of plurality, diversity, and difference. As Disch in her study of Arendt's philosophy observes, Arendt takes the premise from which philosophers have tried to escape, which is that politics begins with a plurality of agents in relation to each other, and transforms it "from an 'intrinsic weakness' of the human condition to a source of uniquely human power" (Disch 1994, 31). Again and again Arendt's conclusion is that what makes our collective action difficult—and in a sense even impossible—is what only makes our collective action possible and real.

In this respect Arendt takes a completely different direction from what Honig refers to as *virtue* theories. While *virtue* theories aim to make political action possible by erasing or at least reducing plurality, Arendt sees it as the main task of political action to make plurality possible. The end and raison d'être of politics, she writes, is "to establish and keep in existence a space where freedom as virtuosity can appear" (Arendt 1977a, 154).

It is important to realize that the space in which freedom can appear—and because "to *be* free and to act are the same" (Arendt 1977a, 153) this is the space in which new beginnings come into the world, where subjects "come into presence" (see Chapter 2)—is an extremely *fragile* space. As Passerin d'Entrèves makes clear, the space of appearance only comes into existence "whenever actors gather together for the purpose of discussing and deliberating about matters of public concern, and it disappears the moment these activities cease" (Passerin d'Entrèves 1994, 77) The space of appearance comes into being, Arendt writes, "wherever men are together in the manner of speech and action" (Arendt 1977b, 199). But unlike the spaces that are the work of our hands, "it does not survive the actuality of the movement which brought it into being, but disappears ... with the disappearance or arrest of the activities themselves" (Arendt 1977b, 199). Wherever people gather together, it is *potentially* there, "but only potentially, not necessarily and not forever" (Arendt 1977b, 199).

The space of appearance can therefore not be taken for granted wherever we are together with others. It is precisely the end and raison d'être of politics to establish and keep in existence a space where freedom as virtuosity can appear. If this is the end and purpose of, and if this space only exists, so we could say, *in* common action, how, then, should we proceed in our common action in order that freedom can appear? How, to put it differently, can we act "in concert" (Arendt) without erasing plurality and difference? And how, on the other hand, is common action possible, given "the simultaneous presence of innumerable perspectives and aspects in which the common world presents itself and for which no common measurement or denominator can ever be devised?" For "though the common world is the common meeting ground of all, those who are present have different locations in it, and the location of one can no more coincide with the location of another than the location of two objects" (Arendt 1977b, 57).

Virtue theories, as we have seen, have a perfectly and deceptively clear answer to this question: We can only act together, we can only act in concert if we have a common ground, a community with a common identity, if, in other words, we establish a rational community. Arendt's answer, on the other hand, remains consistently committed to plurality and freedom. In the next section I follow Lisa Disch's reading of Arendt's ideas about political judgment, which she summarizes under the notion of "visiting" (see Disch 1994).

Visiting

The first thing to keep in mind in understanding the idea of visiting is that although Arendt is as far away from the liberal approach to politics and political action as possible, she does acknowledge that common action is not possible if we simply let plurality exist. Common action is not possible on the basis of *mere* plurality (which is, of course, quite different from saying that it is only possible on the basis of sameness). Arendt's understanding of politics thus clearly implies a rejection of what I want to call "disconnected pluralism."

Implied in her account of the human condition of plurality is the assumption that connection *is* possible, albeit only as a connection-in-difference. Common action under the condition of plurality is therefore not to be conceived of as an agonistic struggle in which beginners simply enforce their own beginnings upon others. Common action requires decision and hence deliberation and judgment. But just as Arendt rejects *pluralism-without-judgment*, she also rejects what I want to call *judgment-without-pluralism*. She rejects, in other words, any form of political judgment that situates itself outside of the web of plurality.[1]

Arendt articulates her ideas on political judgment in a discussion of Kant's *Critique of Judgement* (Arendt 1982). Political judgment, because it is concerned with our being with others, has to be representative. It requires, in other words, a form of generality or, with the word that Arendt prefers, it requires *publicity*, "the testing that arises from contact with other people's thinking" (Arendt 1982, 42). Contrary, however, to the idea of representative thinking as a form of *abstracting* from one's own contingent situation in order to think in the place "of any other man"—which is the position Kant advocated—Arendt approaches representative thinking as a form of *multiperspective understanding* (see Disch 1994, 152–153). For Arendt "it is not abstraction but considered attention to particularity that accounts for 'enlarged thought'" (Disch 1994, 153). Representative thinking is therefore closely connected with particulars, "with the particular conditions of the standpoints one has to go through in order to arrive at one's own 'general standpoint'" (Arendt 1982, 44).

In order to achieve this, the act of judgment must consist of more than thinking and decision. It needs the help of the *imagination*. But unlike Kant, who assumed that imagination is only needed to establish a critical distance that makes it possible to assume a universal standpoint, Arendt argues that we need imagination both for "putting things in their proper distance" *and* for "bridging the abysses to others" (Disch 1994, 157). The latter activity of the imagination in judging is called *visiting*. Visiting, as Disch explains, involves "constructing stories of an event from each of the plurality of perspectives that might have an interest in telling it and"—and this "and" is crucial—"imagining how I would respond as a character in a story very different from my own" (Disch 1994, 158). Visiting is not the same as *parochialism*, which is not to visit at all but to stay at home. Visiting is also different from *tourism*, which is "to ensure that you will have all the comforts of home even as you travel" (Disch 1994, 158–159). Visiting should, however, also be distinguished from *empathy* that, as a form of "assimilationism" is "forcibly to make yourself at home in a place that is not your home by appropriating its customs" (Disch 1994, 159).

The problem with tourism and empathy is that they both tend to erase plurality. The former does so "by an objectivist stance that holds to 'how we do things' as a lens through which different cultures can only appear as other." The latter trades this spectatorial lens "to assume native glasses, identifying with the new culture so as to avoid the discomfort of being in an unfamiliar place" (Disch 1994, 159). Visiting, in contrast, is "being and thinking in my own identity where actually I am not" (Arendt 1977a, 241). It is to think your *own* thoughts but in a story very different from one's own, thereby permitting yourself the "disorientation that is necessary to understanding just how the world looks different to someone else" (Disch 1994, 159).

The innovative character of the idea of visiting, so I wish to argue, does not lie in the fact that visiting differs from tourism. It is clear that any approach to political judgment that doesn't want to erase plurality has to engage itself with others and otherness. It cannot stay safely at home, neither physically nor virtually, in the sense in which the tourist never comes into unfamiliar places because he always already knows what he will find at the end of his journey. The innovating character of visiting lies in the fact that it provides an alternative for *empathy*. To my mind the main problem with empathy is that it assumes that we can simply (and comfortably) take the position of the other, thereby denying both the situatedness of one's own seeing and thinking and that of the other's. Visiting is therefore *not* to see through the eyes of someone else, but to see *with your own eyes* from a position that is *not* your own—or to be more precise, in a story very different from one's own.

The idea of "visiting" provides an indication of Arendt's answer to the question of how we can establish and keep in existence a space where freedom can appear. "Visiting" can bring about a form of "situated generality" that goes beyond tourism and empathy, in that it takes plurality both as its point of departure and as its aim. According to Arendt's ideas the end of plurality is at the very same time the end of the possibility of freedom, that is, the end of the possibility for something uniquely new to come into the world. It is only when we take that which makes our being with others difficult seriously, that there is at least a possibility for this is now beginning to appear, to come into presence, to come into the world of plurality and difference.

How Difficult Should Education Be?

In this chapter I have tried to show that there is a way to think about our being with others in which the fact of plurality is *not* conceived as a problem that must be overcome so that our common action can become possible, but where this fact is seen as that which makes our being with others possible and real in the first place. I have tried to make clear, in other words, that which makes our interaction difficult—and in a sense even impossible—is not a threat to our common action but rather is its internal condition of possibility. I have characterized this as a deconstructive reading of human interaction.

There are two places in Arendt's thought where this deconstructive line of thinking can be seen. The first instance is her claim that the impossibility to remain unique masters of what we do is the very condition under which our beginnings can come into the world. Here she shows that our coming into the world structurally relies on the activities of others to take up our beginnings, yet others will always do so in their own, unpredictable ways. The second instance is to be found in Arendt's contention that freedom only exists *in* action, which, by definition, is action-with-others. We cannot be free if we are alone and isolated; we can only be free when we act. This also means that we can only be free in a worldly space, a space of plurality and difference. We cannot be free in a space that is homogeneous and depluralized. The kind of freedom that we can experience in such a space, so we might say, is a freedom where there is nothing at stake, it is not a "difficult freedom." Arendt's freedom-as-action is only hazardous and hence real in the space where we are with *others*.

The space where new beginnings can come into presence is a space that does not exist independently of our actions. Just as a performance only exists in the performance itself, the space of freedom only exists *in action*, which is, by definition, action with others. When Arendt argues that action is the activity that goes directly between men without the intermediary of things or matter, it is therefore not to highlight some kind of mysterious immaterial quality of action. The point simply is that action doesn't possess any durability or permanence *outside* the realm of action. While institutions are important—and it can, and indeed has been argued that Arendt doesn't pay sufficient attention to the role of such durable structures (see Passerin d'Entrèves 1994)—the point in favor of Arendt is that it is not the mere existence of institutions that guarantees the space in which freedom can appear. What is needed is a constant alertness to the "quality" of action and a persistent commitment to act in such a way that freedom can appear, so that new beginnings can come into the world. I have suggested that visiting is one possible way through which this might be achieved.

If, at this point, we move from the realm of politics to the realm of education, it is first of all important to bear in mind that we should *not* think of politics as a *metaphor* for education. To establish and keep in existence a space where freedom can appear, where new beginnings can come into the world, is not only the end and raison d'être of politics. It is, as I have argued, also the main and ultimate concern of education. As Carsten Ljunggren has put it, education is "not about human nature being repressed or liberated" but "about individuals becoming somebody" (Ljunggren 1999, 55)—which, as we can now say, by necessity takes place through action, through our being with others. Of course, what happens in schools and other institutionalized places of learning, is not focused and is not to be focused exclusively on this process of becoming somebody. It would be a mistake to think that education and schooling can and should be reduced to this. This is not only because education is always also concerned with the acquisition of knowledge, skills, competencies, attitudes, et cetera. But even more because it would be a false dichotomy to think that education can and should *either* be about "becoming somebody" or about learning. It is more to the point to say that we become somebody through the way in which we engage with what we learn.

Given what I have been arguing in this chapter it will therefore be clear that any attempt to make education into a technique, any attempt to conceive of it in terms of instrumentality, poses a threat to the very possibility of becoming somebody *through* education—which, to paraphrase Arendt, eventually will go against "the essentials of education" itself. After all, to make education into a technique requires an erasure of plurality, diversity and difference. It requires an erasure, in other words, of what makes education difficult. For this reason we can say that plurality is not only the condition of human action, but that it is also the condition of education itself. I want to stress one more time that this is not the plurality of the coexistence of separate, disconnected, private spheres. It is a plurality that only exists, that in a sense itself only comes into presence in our being with others. It is a plurality, to put it differently, that only exists in interaction.

This means, in sum, that the difficulty of education is not only the positive condition of possibility of education. Since this difficult is never simply there—the conditions for action have to be achieved again and again—the conclusion can only be that it is the very task and responsibility of education to keep in existence a space in which freedom can appear, a space in which unique, singular individuals can come into the world.

Note

1. At this point I agree with Disch (1994, 71) that Arendt's work is far from an "agonistic celebration of 'greatness,' conceived as an aesthetic disregard for the practical consequences of political action." I also follow Disch in her claim that Arendt is *not* a defender of Enlightenment universalism (which is the "associational" interpretation that Habermas has given of Arendt's work) (see Disch 1994, 72–73). "Visiting" suggests a way that goes beyond these two options.

5

The Architecture of Education

Creating a Worldly Space

What is the role of education today? And what is there to do for educators—for teachers, parents, and all those who have an educational responsibility toward "newcomers"? These are difficult questions, both conceptually and in a practical sense. What do we understand by "education"? What does it mean to have an educational responsibility? Who has an educational responsibility? Where does such a responsibility come from, and what does it entail? And how can we capture and characterize what educational responsibility entails *today*? These questions are not only difficult; they are also urgent. The next generation cannot wait. Yet the most pressing problem might not so much be that of finding an adequate answer to these questions, although this should be done as well. The main problem today might well lie in the fact that there are too many answers. Or to be more precise: that there is too little doubt about what these questions actually mean and what they ask from us. The main problem might well be that these questions are not considered to be difficult at all. There are, after all, clear answers available: The purpose of education is to secure a country's competitiveness in the global economy. The purpose of education today is to transmit the knowledge, values, and dispositions of good citizenship. The purpose of education today is to make sure that students achieve the highest scores on international tests. And so on.

These answers shouldn't be dismissed outright, since they do contain a certain element of truth. There is a connection between the economy and social justice, although it is difficult to see how this can be articulated in terms of competitiveness. Although it might be impossible to define what good citizenship exactly is, there are clear examples of behavior that threatens the well-being of others. And most parents do want their children to do well in school, although a high score on a league table might not necessarily coincide with their values and aspirations. The problem with these answers is therefore not that they are *completely* nonsensical (and their attractiveness lies precisely in the fact that they make some sense). But there are at least two problems with these answers.

The first problem is that these answers are generally presented as self-evident and inevitable. In this respect they exemplify what Zygmunt Bauman has called the TINA creed: There Is No Alternative (Bauman 1999, 98). The TINA creed suggests that there are no value judgments involved in deciding on the role and task of education. The TINA creed suggests that the global economy is simply a reality to which we must adjust out educational efforts, and not something that is actually desired by some to serve particular interests. The TINA creed suggests that decisions about the future of education can simply be derived from international league tables and OECD statistics, without the need for any judgment about the meaning and value of such findings.

The second problem with prevailing ideas about the purpose of education concerns the underlying assumptions about what education is and what it can achieve. "Common sense" thinking about education generally thinks of education as the insertion of newcomers into a particular order. Education is seen in terms of the creation of particular identities—the lifelong learner, the good citizen, the high-achieving student—and in terms of the creation of a competitive, stable, and successful social order. For this to be possible, the educational process itself has to be depicted as a technology, as an instrument that can be put to work to bring about predetermined ends. If the instrument fails, the blame is usually put on students who lack motivation, parents who provide insufficient support, or teachers who lack effective teaching skills—not on the (flawed) assumptions about what education can realistically achieve.

In the preceding chapters I have presented a different way to understand education, one that does not conceive of education as a process of insertion and adaptation or the production of a particular social order but that is concerned with the coming into the world of unique, singular beings. In this chapter I want to explore one more dimension of this alternative view, focusing on the issue of educational responsibility. What does it mean to have such a responsibility? What does such a responsibility entail? And, more importantly, if education cannot be conceived as a technique or an instrument, what is there actually to *do* for educators?

To develop an answer to these questions I will in this chapter explore the parallels between education and architecture through a discussion of the tradition of *Bildung*—sometimes translated into English as "edification"—and the practice of building. I am interested in the educational tradition of *Bildung* because, as I have discussed in the prologue, this tradition, although diverse in its manifestations, has always expressed an interest in the humanity of the human being and thus stands for a way of educational thinking and doing that is significantly different from the near-hegemonic educational discourse today. My question in this chapter will not be how much of the tradition of *Bildung* can be regained or restored today (see also Biesta 2002a, 2002b). I will argue that we should understand the tradition of *Bildung* as a series of contextual responses to particular problems and challenges. From this it follows that the task before us today is *not* that of reproducing the past, but rather that of asking how we should respond educationally to the questions and challenges that are facing us today. In this chapter I will try to identify some of these challenges in order, then, to outline a possible educational response. Following the line of thought presented in the previous chapters, I will suggest that the educational responsibility today has to do with the "creation" of a worldly space, a space of plurality and difference, a space where freedom can appear and where singular, unique individuals can come into the world. To examine what it might mean to create such a space, I will look at how this question has been taken up in recent architectural theory and practice. My conclusion in this chapter will be that both for architects and educators the creation of a worldly space entails a double, deconstructive duty: a duty both for the creation of such spaces and for their constant undoing.

Education and the Tradition of *Bildung*

Can we still relate to the tradition of *Bildung* today, or has this tradition become obsolete and outdated? To answer this question, we need to understand something of the history of the idea of *Bildung*. A brief look at one possible way to understand this history reveals that there is both an *educational* and a *political* dimension to it. On the one hand, as I have briefly discussed in the prologue, *Bildung* stands for an educational ideal that emerged in Greek society and that, through its adoption in Roman culture, humanism, neohumanism, and the Enlightenment, became one of the central notions of the modern Western educational tradition. Central to this tradition is the question of what constitutes an educated or cultivated human being. Generally, the answer to this question was not given in terms of discipline or socialization, that is, in terms of the adaptation to an existing external order. *Bildung* rather referred to the cultivation of the inner life, the cultivation of the human mind or human soul. Initially the question of *Bildung* was approached in terms of the content of *Bildung*: An educated person was someone who had mastered a particular canon. An important step was taken when the acquisition of particular contents became itself recognized as a constitutive aspect of *Bildung*. Since then *Bildung* has always also been understood as self-*Bildung* (see Klafki 1986; Biesta 2002b).

The modern conception of *Bildung* was mainly coined in the Enlightenment when self-*Bildung* became defined in terms of rational autonomy. Kant, as we have seen, provided the classical definition of Enlightenment as "men's [*sic*] release from his self-incurred tutelage [Unmundigkeit] through the exercise of his own understanding" (Kant 1992, 90). Interestingly enough, Kant also argued that "men's vocation and propensity to free thinking" could only be brought about by means of education (see Kant 1982, 701; see also Chapter 2 of this book). He thus placed education at the very center of the Enlightenment, giving educators the task and responsibility of releasing the rationality of human beings in order to make them autonomous. Although Kant saw rational autonomy as a central educational ideal, his educational thinking was intimately connected with a *political* question, namely, the question as to what kind of subjectivity was needed in the emerging civil society of his time and place—Prussia under Frederic the Great. Kant's argument was that civil society needed subjects who could think for themselves and were capable of making their own judgments.

What we can learn from this brief glimpse at the history of the idea of *Bildung* is that, particularly in its modern, Enlightenment configuration, *Bildung* is closely interwoven with political questions and a particular political constellation. *Bildung* should be understood as a "response" to a "question"—we might even say an educational response to a political question. This is a helpful way to understand the tradition of *Bildung,* because it suggests that if we want to relate to this tradition today, we should not so much ask how much *Bildung* is still possible today or how much of the tradition of *Bildung* can be regained or restored. We rather need to ask what kind of problems we are faced with today. What is it that summons our response? What is it that summons our *educational* response? And what is it that summons our educational response *today*? Let me try to give at least a partial answer to this question.

Where Are We, Today?

The first aspect of the situation we find ourselves in today that I wish to highlight has to do with the fact that we live in a world in which the idea of the universal, of universal values and universal truth, has become problematized. The point here is *not* to say that we live in a plural world, because when we look at the history of humankind there has always been plurality. What has changed is the way in which this plurality is understood and approached. What has been put into question is the idea that it is possible to see, overview, describe, and conceptualize this plurality from a neutral point outside of it. One way to describe what is at stake is in terms of the distinction between *diversity* and *difference* (see Bhabha 1990; Säfström and Biesta 2001). Diversity stands for the attempt to see plurality as a set of variations against an identical background or a set of positions within an overarching framework. An example of this is to think of plurality in terms of cultural variations of an underlying universal human nature. What is suggested by such a view is that we are all basically the same and that our differences are "merely cultural." The problem with such a view, as Homi Bhabha makes clear, is that "the universalism that paradoxically permits diversity masks ethnocentric norms, values and interests" (Bhabha 1990, 208) and "doesn't generally recognise the universalist and normative stance from which it constructs its cultural and political judgements" (Bhabha 1990, 209).

Difference, on the other hand, takes the fact that we differ just as we encounter and experience it—which more often than not will mean as it confronts us. What is implied in the latter approach is the recognition that any attempt to locate, understand, and make sense of difference by placing it in an overarching framework can only be done from one of the positions within such a framework—which already shows that the framework itself is not overarching, just as the position is not simply within the framework. To take difference seriously means that we have to give up the idea that we can and should understand and know otherness and difference before we can adequately engage with it. It is to give up the idea that knowledge of the other is a necessary and sufficient condition for engaging with the other. Difference requires a different attitude toward plurality and otherness, one in which the idea of responsibility is more appropriate than the idea of knowledge, one in which ethics is more important than epistemology.

The second dimension I wish to highlight is the fact that we live in a world in which the idea that we can know the essence of what it is to be human has been put into question. Philosophically, as I have discussed in Chapter 2, this questioning has been expressed as a critique of humanism, the attempt to determine "the essence of man [sic]" (Heidegger 1993, 225). To give up the idea that we can know the essence of the human being is, of course, not without danger, because it lets in a wide range of different options, definitions, and manifestations of humanity. The point of the critique of humanism is, however, not to say that all manifestations of humanness are simply and automatically good and desirable. The only point of the critique of humanism is that we cannot know this in advance and that there might be greater danger in foreclosing opportunities for being human than in keeping our options open. This does not mean that there is no judgment involved or required. It only means that the judgment has to come *after* the manifestation and experience of new and different ways of being human.

It is important to see that the critique of humanism is not exclusively motivated by philosophical concerns. We are living in the shadow of an era in which genocide was motivated and justified by a definition of what a real human being was supposed to be. And closer to home we can witness how decisions about abortion and euthanasia are often based on definitions of what a humane life is supposed to look like. Humanism, the claim to know what the humanity of human beings consists of, has thus become a matter of life and death. This is the most important reason to be suspicious of humanism, to be suspicious of any attempt to define for others and before life even begins where the dividing line between the human and the inhuman lies.

The third aspect I wish to highlight is the fact that we live in an era of globalization. It is important to see what globalization is and what it is not. Globalization has nothing to do with the creation of a level playing field. Globalization is a highly asymmetrical process; it is a process in which some practices and activities become incorporated into the logic of others. Globalization is the hegemonic extension of particular networks and practices. Globalization is about the creation of interdependence and at the same time about the creation of new dependencies. In this respect we might even say that globalization is the contemporary face of colonialism.

Globalization takes place in several different spheres. The most prominent one is without doubt the economic sphere. Production, consumption, and finance have all become part of one global network. Although the network is global, it is mainly steered by Western powers, such as OPEC, the OECD, and the G8. As a result, their interests are much better served by the global economy than the interests of those working on the other side of the global economy. The globalization of communication and the media and the globalization of popular culture are closely interwoven with the interests of global capitalism. It is not so much motivated by a commitment to

establish democratic cosmopolitanism, as by the need to create ever newer markets for software and hardware and for
the products of the global entertainment industry. There is,
however, one dimension of globalization that seems to work in
the opposite direction, which is the globalization of ecological
problems. While global capitalism results in the concentration
of wealth in one part of the world, the ecological problems
caused by global production tend to end up in those places
where the economy is weakest and where, for reasons of sheer
economic survival, environmental regulations are minimal.

Educationally the most striking feature of global capitalism
is that it "produces" a particular kind of subjectivity or, to
be more precise, that it is mainly interested in one possible
subject-position, namely, that of the subject as consumer. The
ideal consumer is the "dedicated follower of fashion," the
subject who lets his or her wants be defined by the need of
capitalist production for constant expansion. Global capitalism is not interested in individual differences—other, that is,
than for the creation of new niche markets or the invention
of new trends and fashions—nor is it interested in different modes or models of subjectivity. In this respect, global
capitalism threatens the opportunities for different ways of
being a subject, different ways of leading one's life and being
human. It tends to make one contingent subject position—the
subject as consumer—into something that is inevitable and
almost has become natural; a mode of subjectivity for which
there is no alternative. The fact that shopping has become
one of the most meaningful activities in the lives of many
people is evidence of the way in which the subject-position
"suggested" by global capitalism has been internalized and
"naturalized."

Bildung: Creating a Worldly Space

How should we approach the question of the humanity of
human beings in the face of these challenges? And what

kind of educational response would follow from this? Let me return to the three challenges in reverse order.

I have argued that global capitalism is only interested in one mode of subjectivity, that of the subject as consumer. More than simply an interest, global capitalism actively promotes this subject position through a range of different operations and strategies. Global capitalism is not interested in what makes individuals singular and unique, other, that is, than in terms of lifestyle. But from the point of view of consumption all individuals are interchangeable; it does not matter *who* consumes, as long as there are sufficient consumers. If, following a key dimension of the tradition of *Bildung*, we see our educational responsibility as a responsibility for the humanity of the human being, it is clear that we should resist the suggestion that all human beings are simply interchangeable units. In response to the not-so-hidden agenda of global capitalism, we need to understand our educational responsibility as a responsibility for the singularity and uniqueness of *each* individual human being.

This brings us to the discussion about humanism. The problem with humanism, as I have argued, stems from its desire to define what the humanity of the human beings consists of. "Strong" forms of humanism, which claim to know the real essence of the human being, clearly impede different ways of being human. The problem with humanism is, however, not only that it restricts different modes and models of subjectivity, but also that it does so in advance of any manifestation of subjectivity. The educational response has to be one of openness: an openness toward new and different ways of being human. This response must therefore be experimental and experiential. The question of the humanity of human beings has to be taken up as a practical question, a question that requires a response with every new manifestation of subjectivity, with the arrival of every newcomer.

This is not to say, of course, that any manifestation must simply be accepted. Subjectivity is not a kind of inner self that merely awaits expression. As I have shown in the previous chapters, we can only come into presence, we can only come into the world as a result of the ways in which others respond to us. It is, as Arendt puts it so well, the "impossibility to remain unique masters of what [we] do," which is the one and only condition under which our beginnings can come into the world (Arendt 1977b, 220). This is why a concern for the coming into the world of new beginnings and new beginners does not entail the mere acceptance of any new beginning. It rather entails a concern for the dynamics and complexities of the social fabric in which newcomers begin, that is, a recognition of the fact that we always act upon beings who are not only capable of their own actions but whose coming into the world depends as much on our response as our coming into the world depends on their responses. *This* is the predicament of human action, and there is no easy way out. What is needed, again and again, is "fresh" judgment.

If we bring these points together and ask how we can connect with the tradition of *Bildung* understood as being concerned with the humanity of human beings in response to the challenges we are faced with today, it becomes clear that the educational responsibility must indeed focus on the coming into the world of unique, singular beings. It is not about the production of particular identities or subjectivities through the application of educational technology, or about the creation of social order through particular educational interventions. It is important not to forget, however, that the world is not a neutral place. The world, as the space in which freedom can appear (Arendt), is by necessity a world of plurality and difference. This means, however, that educational responsibility, the responsibility of the educator, is not only a responsibility for "newcomers"—it is at the very same time a responsibility for the world. It is a responsibility to create and keep in existence a "worldly space" through which new beginnings can come into presence.

Yet how do we do this? What does it involve to create and keep in existence a "worldly space," a space of otherness and difference? Is such an act of creation possible, or is this again asking for an educational technology? To find an answer to these questions—or at least to understand what is entailed in asking these questions—I now want to turn to the field of architecture in order to see what we can learn from those whose main concern is precisely with the creation of space.

Building: Creating a Worldly Space

What is the relationship between buildings and their use? Can buildings control their use, and hence can architects control the uses of the spaces they design? And if so, is this the proper task of architecture? It will not come as a surprise that there is no agreement among architects about the answers to these questions and that ideas have also changed over time. Some architects do indeed believe that it is their task to create spaces that prescribe a certain (proper) use. Modern architecture has seen many examples of the desire to change society through architecture, motivated either by conservative or progressive agendas. As Diane Ghirardo argues, the Modern Movement in architecture was characterized by a passionate belief in the "power of form to transform the world" and in the idea that social problems could be solved through the "right" architecture (Ghirardo 1996, 9). It is important to see that this tendency is not simply a thing of the past. Up to the present day architects and urban planners are "trying to get it right" or at least are trying not to repeat the design and planning mistakes of the past. In all this we shouldn't doubt the good intentions of architects who want to make a difference. Yet there is an extremely thin line between the desire to address social problems through architecture and the creation of new forms of surveillance and control that limit the opportunities for human action.

Mossbourne Community Academy

A telling example of the latter can be found in Mossbourne Community Academy, a new inner-city comprehensive in

Hackney, East London, England. The school, one of the first public-private partnership schools in England, was designed by celebrated architect Richard Rogers, in close collaboration with headmaster Michael Wilshaw. Their aim was "to create an environment in which children will flourish" (Neill 2004, 39). But what does this laudable idea mean in practice? In Mossbourne there is no single staff room, so that staff are not removed from students. Instead they have dedicated spaces spread throughout the building to make them both visible and accessible to children. The school has no corridors, because, according to the headmaster, corridors are where most bullying takes place. And there are glass walls to the front and back of every classroom, so that everyone can see what is going on from any vantage point in the school. The headmaster sums it all up as follows: "If I had a blank piece of paper I would design a school where you can easily monitor the nooks and crannies, where everything that's going on can be easily monitored...a space where kids can't be spotted, or teachers feel isolated, doesn't work. Here, from wherever I stand, I can see the children" (Neill 2004, 39).

This is where the functionalism of modern architecture becomes problematic and where, in this particular example, the desire to create an environment in which children will flourish turns into a surveillance machine where "appropriate behavior" is secured because everyone and everything is visible from the central point of surveillance. This doesn't just remind us of Bentham's Panopticon; it *is* a modern-day Panopticon (see Foucault 1995, 195–228).

Alfred Lerner Hall

Is it possible for architects to overcome functionalism? As I briefly discussed in Chapter 2, the work of the Swiss architect Bernard Tschumi aims precisely to deal with the challenge of functionalism. In his theoretical work Tschumi has challenged the traditional notion of architecture as the art of "pinning things down," of "fixing things" (Tschumi 1994a, 10). He has challenged the functionalist conception of architecture, which rests upon the model of efficiency, that is, on the assumption that there is and must be "a seamless coincidence between space and its use," where "the building...must 'work,' answering to its designated use" (Tschumi 1994a, 10). Tschumi's suggestion is that we shouldn't think of architecture as only having to do with the creation of space, but that we should include the *usage* of space in our conception of architecture. This is why he advocates a definition of architecture of "simultaneously space and event" (Tschumi 1994b, 23). Instead of understanding the noncoincidence between form and meaning, between space and use as a failure, Tschumi argues that architecture's strength precisely lies in this "point of noncoincidence, of disjunction, of failure...between the (supposed) cause-and-effect relations of...use and space" (Tschumi 1994a, 11).

Tschumi's suggestions are not only important for overcoming functionalism and its excesses. By including events—which, by definition are unpredictable and incalculable—into his definition of architecture, he hints at a form of architecture that is open to the manifestation of different forms of subjectivity, different ways of coming into the world. But two issues remain. The first point is that Tschumi's conception of architecture does not necessarily result in a worldly space, a space of encounter with and exposure to otherness and difference. Although his definition may help architects to resist the temptation to "get it right," the buildings they design and the spaces they create using this definition could still end up being used as monocultural spaces. It seems, therefore, that something more is required. The second question with regard to Tschumi's proposals is whether they actually make any difference in architectural practice. What does it actually mean for an architect to design a space on the basis of the idea that architecture is both space and event?

There is a real question as to whether Tschumi's own buildings live up to the expectations set by his theoretical work. The key idea in his design for the Alfred Lerner Hall, the student center of Columbia University–New York, is the inclusion of a range of corridors and corridor-like spaces into the building (see Tschumi 2001). The explicit purpose of these spaces is to facilitate encounters. Although Tschumi doesn't want to control these encounters—neither their occurrence nor their "content"—and in this respect has indeed tried to create a space in which events can occur—there is still a trace of functionalism in his approach, in that he has tried to design for the *possibility* of encounters to occur. We could call this approach a form of *negative functionalism*, in that it is not aimed at trying to prescribe how a building should be used and how the users should behave, but instead aims *not* to make some actions and events *im*possible. What is more difficult to see in this particular building is the extent to which it succeeds in catering for the "real" event, that is, the real transgression of the architectural agenda. Is the Alfred Lerner Hall a worldly space? Is it used as a worldly space? Is it a space of plurality and difference? Part of the problem with this particular building might well lie in its location, something for which Tschumi may not be held completely responsible. Although this building will definitely facilitate encounters, we shouldn't forget that these will only be encounters between those who have managed to pass the entrance of Columbia University, both literally and metaphorically. Columbia University student center is, after all, part of a high-security campus of a wealthy North American university, which means that many encounters, events, and transgression are precluded from the outset.

Montessori College Oost

The question of the creation of worldly spaces also plays a central role in the work of the Dutch architect Herman Hertzberger. An important distinction in Hertzberger's work is that between collective space and social space.

What distinguishes social space from collective space is encounter and interaction. "It is social contact that turns collective space into social space" (Hertzberger 2000, 135). Collective spaces such as churches and mosques are almost exclusively organized around a central point where the message is proclaimed. In theaters and auditoriums the attention is likewise centrally orientated. In all these situations "there is an all-inclusive construct that encourages a shared concentration and a harmony among those attending certain organized events" (Hertzberger 2000, 135). Although collective space definitely has a function in society, Hertzberger emphasizes the need for another kind of space that is "not just targeted at one and the same activity" but is "organized" in such a way "that everyone can behave in accordance with their own intentions and movements and so be given the opportunity to seek out their own space in relation to others there" (Hertzberger 2000, 135). This is the quality usually identified with the street or the city. City for Hertzberger is "the model for society"; it is "our universe and arena where we show ourselves in company, sound out social situations, measure ourselves against others" (Hertzberger 2000, 120). Hertzberger's conception of the city thus comes close to the idea of a worldly space, a space of encounter and difference. For Hertzberg "city" is the space where we "are continually preoccupied with measuring, mirroring and pitting ourselves against each other" because "it is not we that determine who we are, but mainly others" (Hertzberger 2000, 120). The "aim" of the city is therefore "to provide the opportunity for us to inspect, assess, keep an eye on and bump into one another" (Hertzberger 2000, 120).

It is important to see that for Hertzberger the city is primarily a *metaphor* for what I call a worldly space. Hertzberger not only makes the point that "public" and "private" are relative concepts, which means that existing cities are not by definition public, social spaces. He also emphasizes that architects "must keep striving with architectural and urbanistic means to uphold the openness of the private 'bastions' and the continuity of the street so that the collective doesn't get reduced in the interest of consolidating the private" (Hertzberger 2000, 134). What Hertzberger is most concerned about are the quasi-public spaces such as the shopping mall and the high-security university campus—spaces that might look public but actually are organized around private interests, limiting and restricting encounter and transgression. This is why Hertzberger advocates that buildings that are used collectively should be organized "more like cities" (Hertzberger 2000, 137) and it is here that he sees a prime responsibility for the architect.

Hertzberger argues that "it takes a conscious, purposeful attitude on the part of designers to give the space inside a building...the quality of social space" (Hertzberger 2000, 156). But this in itself is not enough. "If a building is to function properly, it is essential that it is organized so that people do indeed encounter one another" (Hertzberger 2000, 156). Like the designers of Mossbourne Academy, Hertzberger stresses the importance of visibility, of "strategic sight lines" and "transparency." But unlike Mossbourne Academy, Hertzberger's concern is not for a Panopticon, where everything and everyone is visible and overseeable from the center. For him visibility has to do with "visible relationships and possibilities for encountering or avoiding others" (Hertzberger 2000, 156). He therefore concludes that "we must keep searching for space forms that make our buildings mechanisms where everyone crosses everyone else's path" (Hertzberger 2000, 172).

In my view Hertzberger is not only more perceptive about the issues involved in the creation of worldly spaces than Tschumi is, I also believe that some of his buildings have been more successful in meeting this challenge. One of his most recent buildings is "Montessori College Oost," a school for intermediate-level vocational education in Amsterdam. The school houses some 1,200 pupils, 95 percent of whom come from roughly fifty different countries (see Bergers 2003, 231). The most striking feature of the school building is the large atrium with balconies and balustrades, which is dissected by numerous staircase bridges. There are stairs, steps, and benches that serve as seating and writing areas in almost every corner of the building. The first experiences with the use of the building suggest that Hertzberger has indeed managed to create a building in which everyone crosses everyone else's path, a building with what he calls "urban qualities," with opportunities for encounters, for use, and events. The balconies and staircases create many sight lines and hence opportunities for visual relationships. According to school director Nico Moen one of the effects of the extensive sight lines is "that pupils show a greater respect for each other and also exercise a certain control over each other in a positive way" (Bergers 2003, 231). Interestingly enough, the only spaces without such visibility—the toilets—were subject to dirtying and vandalism and were the scene of disputes. The "solution" for this problem has been to remove the doors to the lobbies. Although Moen is not entirely happy with this solution, he sees it as part "of a constant struggle to find a balance between supervision and privacy"—which he considers to be a key educational principle underlying both the Montessori approach and the design of this particular building.

Conclusion: The Paradox of *Bildung*/Building

The conclusion that can be drawn from these examples is that it is not possible for architects to escape functionalism completely. The only way out, of course, is not to build anything at all, but this would mean the end of architecture. This is what we might call the dilemma of the architect and the paradox of architecture. If architects want to escape functionalism, if they want to give up the desire to control, they have to give up architecture; if, however, architects want to be architects, if they want to take up the responsibility of the architect, they have to be functionalists in one way or another. Both options, in a sense, betray the responsibility of the architect, or at least the responsibility of the architect who doesn't want to control the way in which people use their buildings. Yet the way out of this dilemma—which might better be described as a way "in"—is not to choose for one of the options, but rather to take the contradiction seriously and to give it a central place in one's understanding of what it means to be an architect. The duty of the architect—which, following Derrida (1992, 80) I want to call a double duty—is precisely to be committed to both spaces and events, to both design and the transgression of design, to both building and its undoing.

This, so I wish to argue, is not different for educators. In this and the preceding chapters I have argued that education, as distinguished from socialization, that is, from the insertion of newcomers into an existing order, entails a responsibility for the coming into the world of unique, singular beings. This is not something that can be understood in a technical manner because there is no technology that will produce unique, singular beings. But if it is the case that the condition under which individuals can come into the world as unique, singular beings is the existence of worldly spaces, of spaces of plurality and difference, then it means that the responsibility of the educator is first and foremost a responsibility for the creation of such worldly spaces, space with "urban quality," as Hertzberg would put it. The paradox is that the "worldliness" of such spaces cannot be produced in any technical way either. As I have outlined in Chapter 3, the community of those who have nothing in common—which can be read as a definition of the worldliness of worldly spaces—only exists in the *interruption* of the rational community, the community of logic, rationality, order, structure, and purpose. But this does not mean that educators shouldn't do anything at all, because that would mean giving up their educational responsibility as well. The responsibility of the educator, so I wish to suggest, lies precisely in a concern for the paradoxical—or

115

deconstructive—combination of *education and its undoing*. As I concluded in Chapter 3, educators and teachers should be aware that what disrupts the smooth operation of the rational community is not necessarily a disturbance of the educational process, but might well be the very point at which students begin to find their own, unique, responsive, and responsible voice. This also shows that the responsibility of the educator, the educational responsibility, is a responsibility for something that cannot be known in advance—it is a responsibility *without* knowledge of what one is responsible for.

6
_____

Education and the
Democratic Person

In the foregoing chapters I have presented a different way
to understand and approach education, one that isn't based
on a truth about the human being, one that doesn't claim to
know what the humanity of the human being consists of,
and one that doesn't think of education as the production of
particular identities or subjectivities or the insertion of newcomers into an existing social order. Instead I have argued for
an approach that focuses on the multifarious ways in which
human beings as unique, singular individuals come into the
world. I have argued that we come into the world as unique,
singular beings through the ways in which we take up our
responsibility for the otherness of the others, because it is
in those situations that we speak with our own "voice" and
not with the representative voice of the rational community.
I have shown that the world in which we come into presence
is a world of plurality and difference, because we can only
come into the world if others, who are not like us, take up
our beginnings in such a way that they can bring their beginnings into the world as well. I have therefore argued that
the educational responsibility is not only a responsibility for
the coming into the world of unique and singular beings; it
is also a responsibility for the world as a world of plurality

and difference. The creation of such a world, the creation of a worldly space, is not something that can be done in a straightforward manner. It rather entails a "double duty" for the creation of worldly spaces and for their undoing. Along these lines I have tried to articulate a way to understand education that itself responds to the challenges we are faced with today, including the disappearance of a language of education in the age of learning.

In this chapter I want to show how this different way to understand and approach education might make a difference. I focus on one of the central questions of modern education: the role of education in a democratic society. In what follows I present an understanding of democratic education that doesn't think of democratic education in terms of the production of democratic citizens, but rather reconfigures democracy and democratic education around the key concepts and ideas that I have put forward in this book.

Democracy and Education Revisited

Questions about democracy have always been closely intertwined with questions about education. Ever since its inception in the *polis* of Athens, political and educational thinkers alike have asked what kind of education would best prepare the people (*demos*) for their participation in the ruling (*kratos*) of their society. Although our complex global world bears little or no resemblance to the *polis* of Athens, the question of the relationship between education and democracy is as important and urgent today as it was then. In new and emerging democracies schools are considered to have a pivotal role to play in the formation of a democratic citizenry and the creation of a democratic culture. In old and established democracies education is seen as central to the preservation of democratic life and is nowadays often called upon to counter political apathy, particularly among the young. The increasing marketization of education and the subsequent loss of democratic control over schools is a further reason why in many countries around the world questions about the relationship between education and democracy are high on the agenda again (see, for example, Torres 1998; Saltman 2000; McLaughlin 2000; McDonnell et al. 2000; McNeil 2002; Wells, Slayton, and Scott 2002; Biesta 2004a).

But how should we understand the relationship between democracy and education? And what is the role of schools in a democratic society? In this chapter I argue that an answer to these questions crucially depends on our views about the democratic person (see also Westheimer and Kahne 2004). Stated in more philosophical terms: It depends on our ideas about the kind of subjectivity that is considered to be desirable or necessary for a democratic society. One influential line of thinking holds that democracy needs rational individuals who are capable of making their own free and independent judgments. This idea, which was first formulated by Enlightenment philosophers more than two centuries ago and has remained influential up to the present day (see, for example, Rawls 1993; 1997; Habermas 1996; Dryzek 2000), has led to the belief that it is the task of schools to "create" or "produce" such individuals. It has promoted the idea that schools should make children "ready for democracy" by instilling in them the knowledge, skills, and dispositions that will turn them into democratic citizens.

There are, however, several problems with this view of democratic education. The first is that this way of thinking rests upon an *instrumentalistic* conception of democratic education, one in which education is seen as an instrument for bringing about democracy—and hence as the institution that can conveniently be blamed if it fails to do so. The problem here is that schools are maneuvered into a position in which they seem to have to carry the whole responsibility for the future of democracy (and we all know how easily politicians point the finger at education when there are problems with democracy). It is not only not fair to burden schools with this task; it is also unrealistic to assume that schools can "make or break" democracy. The second problem with the idea of education as the "production" of the democratic person is that it entails an *individualistic approach to democratic education,* one in which the educational efforts are focused on equipping individuals with the proper set of democratic knowledge, skills, and dispositions, without asking questions about their relationships with others and about the social and political context in which they learn and act. This is closely connected to the third problem, which is that this view of democratic education rests upon an *individualistic view of democracy itself,* one in which it is assumed that the success of democracy depends on the knowledge, skills, and dispositions of individuals and on their willingness as individuals to act democratically. What is particularly problematic here is the assumption that democracy is only possible if all citizens are "properly" educated and act accordingly. The question this raises is whether we take democracy seriously enough if we assume that it can only exist if it is founded on a common identity. Isn't it the case that the challenge of democracy lies precisely in our ability to live together with those who are not like us (see Säfström and Biesta 2001)?

In this chapter I wish to advance a different understanding of democratic education, one that is *not* centered around the idea that democratic education is about the "production" of the democratic person, one that does *not* conceive of the democratic person as an isolated individual with a predefined set of knowledge, skills, and dispositions, and one in which it is acknowledged that democracy is about plurality and difference, not identity and sameness. I wish to explore, in other words, whether it is possible to overcome the instrumentalism and individualism that is characteristic of the idea of democratic education as the "production" of the democratic person. I believe that it is important to challenge such an understanding of democratic education, not only because of the unrealistic expectations it raises about what schools can actually achieve, but also because of the fact that it puts the burden for the future of democracy too much on schools and too little on society at large. The focus of this chapter is on a discussion of three conceptions of the democratic person: an individualistic, a social, and a political conception of democratic subjectivity. I argue that the latter view, which takes its inspiration mainly from Hannah Arendt and builds upon ideas presented in previous chapters, provides us with a way to overcome the instrumentalism and individualism in the theory and practice of democratic education. I also argue that such a view can help us to be more realistic about what can be expected from schools and other institutionalized places of education and can help us to be clearer about what should be expected from society at large. I conclude that schools can neither create nor save democracy. They can only support societies in which democratic action and democratic subjectivity are real possibilities.

Defining Democracy

Any discussion about democracy raises questions about its definition. Although the literal meaning of democracy is not difficult to grasp—rule (*kratos*) by the people (*demos*)—many different interpretations of what democracy might mean have been put forward over time (see, for example, Held 1987; 1995; Gutmann 1993; Mouffe 1992). These interpretations not only differ in their answers to the questions of what ruling actually means (for example, direct participation or indirect representation) and who should be considered to be "the people" (for example free men, landowners, women, children, all human beings), they also differ in their justification of the ideal of democracy, ranging from democracy as the optimal context for human flourishing to Winston Churchill's definition of democracy as "the worst form of government except all those other forms that have been tried" (Shapiro 2003, 148).

One of the main problems with the ideal of democracy is that it has become a concept that not many people do not want to be associated with. As Held correctly observes, "nearly everyone today says they are democrats, no matter whether their views are on the left, centre or right" (Held 1987, 1). There exists, therefore, a real danger that democracy has so many meanings that it has ceased to have any meaning at all. In response to this, some have argued that we should understand democracy as an "essentially contested concept" (Gallie 1955), that is, a concept whose meaning is constantly challenged and disputed, not because people cannot agree on its definition, but because the very idea of democracy calls for a continuous discussion about and reappraisal of what it actually means and entails. This is what John Dewey had in mind when he wrote that the very idea of democracy "has to be constantly discovered, and rediscovered, remade and reorganized" (Dewey 1987a [1937], 182). How then, should we define democracy?

We could use Abraham Lincoln's broad definition of democracy as "the government of the people, by the people, and for the people" (Lincoln, quoted in Torres 1998, 159). Beetham and Boyle, in their book on democracy commissioned by UNESCO, suggest a slightly more precise definition of democracy as entailing "the twin principles of *popular control* over collective decisionmaking and *equality of rights* in the exercise of that control" (Beetham and Boyle 1995, 1). Their definition embodies the ideal that decisions that affect an association as a whole should be made by all its members, and that each should have an equal right in taking part in such decision making. In doing so, their definition hints at Dewey's insight that democracy is "more than a form of government," but that it is "primarily a mode of associated living" (Dewey 1966, 87). Such a social conception of democracy (Festenstein 1997) acknowledges that democracy is not exclusively about collective decision making in the political domain, but that it has to do with participation in the "construction, maintenance and transformation" of social and political life more generally (see Bernstein 2000, xxi; Barber 1984; 1998). A social conception of democracy expresses, in other words, that democracy is about inclusive ways of social and political action.

If this suffices as a working definition of democracy, how, then, can the relationship between democracy and education be understood? I will refer to the two most prevalent answers to this question as "education *for* democracy" and "education *through* democracy."

Education for Democracy

The most common way in which the relationship between democracy and education is understood, is one in which the role of education is seen as that of *preparing* children—and "newcomers" more generally—for their future participation in democratic life. In this approach the role of democratic education is considered to be threefold: (1) to teach about democracy and democratic processes (the *knowledge* component), (2) to facilitate the acquisition of democratic skills such as deliberation, collective decision making, and dealing with difference (the *skills* component), and (3) to support the acquisition of a positive attitude toward democracy (the *disposition* or *values* component).

Many educationalists and politicians indeed believe that schools and other educational institutions have a crucial role to play in preparing the next generation for their participation in democracy. We can find this line of thinking expressed in such book titles as *Schooling for Democracy* (Giroux 1989), *Educating the Democratic Mind* (Parker 1995), *Creating Citizens* (Callan 1997), and *Developing Democratic Character in the Young* (Soder et al., 2001). Amy Gutmann, in her *Democratic Education* (1987), also exemplifies this view when she defines political education as a process of "the cultivation of the virtues, knowledge, and skills necessary for political participation" and argues that the purpose of political education is that it "*prepares* citizens to participate in consciously reproducing their society" (Gutmann 1987, 287; emphasis added).

There can be no doubt that the preparation of children and other newcomers for their role in democracy is an important task for schools and other educational institutions (although, as I will argue in what follows, there are important questions to be asked about the exact nature of such "preparation"). One of the key issues in recent debates is whether schools should actively *promote* democracy (the disposition or values component), or whether they should only focus on the teaching of knowledge about democracy and the acquisition of democratic skills (the knowledge and skills components). Carr and Hartnett in their book on democratic education argue that the primary aim of education for democracy should be "to ensure that all future citizens are equipped with the knowledge, values, and skills of deliberative reasoning minimally necessary for their participation in the democratic life of their society" (Carr and Hartnett 1996, 192). Gutmann takes the similar view that "a society that supports conscious social reproduction must educate all educable children to be *capable* of participating in collectively shaping their society" (Gutmann 1987, 39; emphasis added). Both, therefore, appear to refrain from the idea that schools should actively promote democracy and democratic values.

Education through Democracy

Although there are many good reasons for supporting the thrust of education *for* democracy, there is a limit to what can be achieved by means of deliberate attempts to teach democracy. As research on political socialization has shown, students not only learn from what they are being taught; they also learn—and often learn more and learn more strongly—from many of the other situations in which they take part (see, for example, Torney-Purta et al. 2001). Schools might have exemplary curricula for the teaching of democracy and citizenship, but if the internal organization of a school is undemocratic, this will undoubtedly have a negative impact on students' attitudes and dispositions toward democracy.

It is for precisely this reason that many educators have argued that the best way to educate *for* democracy is *through* democracy, that is, by means of democratic forms of education. In their *Democratic Schools* (1995) Apple and Beane explain that democratic schooling entails both the creation of "democratic structures and processes by which life in the school is carried out," and the creation of "a curriculum that will give young people democratic experiences" (Apple and Beane 1995, 9). The examples they provide reveal that democratic schooling is possible, although it definitely isn't easy. It requires a continuous attention for the democratic quality of the school and the learning environment more generally. Apple and Beane emphasize that it is "in the details of everyday life," and not "in the glossy political rhetoric" that "the most powerful meaning of democracy is formed" (Apple and Beane 1995, 103).

Schooling *through* democracy can thus be seen as a specific way of schooling *for* democracy, one in which it is maintained that the best way to prepare for democracy is through participation in democratic life itself. This argument extends, of course, to life outside the walls of the school. Although the school occupies an important place in the lives of young people, they also live and learn at home, on the street, as consumers, as Internet users, and so on (see Biesta and Lawy 2006). From an educational point of view it is, therefore, also important to raise questions about the democratic quality of these environments. It is with this in mind that proponents of participatory forms of democracy have argued that "the major function of participation in the theory of participatory democracy is...an educative one" (Pateman 1970, 42). The assumption here is that the experience of participation indeed "will develop and foster the democratic personality" (Pateman 1970, 64).

Democracy as a Problem for Education?

Although there are significant differences between "education *for* democracy" and "education *through* democracy," they are similar in at least one respect, in that both focus on how best to prepare children and young people for their future participation in democracy. By focusing on the *preparation of individuals*—either by equipping them with the "right" set of knowledge, skills, and dispositions or by fostering the qualities of the democratic personality in them—both approaches seek to give an answer to the question of how the democratic person can best be created or engendered. In this respect both education *for* democracy and education *through* democracy display instrumentalism and individualism in their approach to democratic education. One way of putting this is to say that both approaches conceive of democracy *as a problem for education,* a problem that is "given" to educators, that is defined elsewhere, and for which educators, schools, and other educational institutions have to provide a solution (and, as I said before, can thus be blamed if things go wrong with democracy).

The question is, however, whether this is the only possible way to understand the role of education in a democratic society. I wish to suggest that how we answer this question depends on our views about the democratic person. In the next sections I will present three different answers to the question of what constitutes the democratic subject: Immanuel Kant's *individualistic* conception of the democratic person, John Dewey's *social* conception, and Hannah Arendt's *political* conception. I will argue that Kant's individualistic view indeed leads to the conclusion that education should "produce" the democratic individual. Dewey's social conception acknowledges that the democratic person cannot be created in isolation but can only emerge through participation in democratic life. Although Dewey has a social conception of the democratic person, his view of democratic education, however, is still characterized by instrumentalism and individualism. Arendt's political conception of democratic subjectivity makes it possible to go beyond the idea of education as the producer and the safeguard of democracy.

Immanuel Kant: An Individualistic Conception of the Democratic Person

Kant's philosophy has its roots in the European Enlightenment. Enlightenment thinkers like Kant responded to the changing political situation in those European countries that were in transition from absolutist rule toward more democratic forms of government (most notably Prussia, France, and Scotland). This raised questions about the qualities that would be needed for people to be effective citizens in civil society. It raised questions, in other words, about the kind of subjectivity needed to make democracy possible. The answer Enlightenment philosophers gave was that a democratic society needs individuals who can make up their own minds and who can think for themselves. Kant captured this very well when he described the motto of the Enlightenment as *"Sapere aude!"*—have the courage to exercise your own understanding (see Kant 1992, 90).

Kant's answer to the question about the kind of subjectivity needed in a democracy focused on the ability of individuals to make use of their own reason without direction from another. This already reveals the individualistic tendency in Kant's conception of the democratic person. For Kant, the democratic person is the one who can think for himself, who can make his own judgments without being led by others. The Kantian subject is therefore a rational subject and an autonomous subject, and it is the task of democratic education to release the rational potential of the human subject.

As I have argued before, Kant's ideas of subjectivity as rational autonomy has had a huge impact on modern educational theory and practice. There are, for example, direct lines from Kant to the work of Piaget and Kohlberg, whose theories of cognitive and moral development build upon Kant's epistemology and moral philosophy, respectively. The idea of rational autonomy is also a guiding principle for liberal education and plays a central role in discussions about critical thinking as an educational ideal. Some even argue that rational autonomy is not simply an educational aim, but that it is the one and only aim of all education (for a critical discussion of this idea, see Biesta and Stams 2001). Kant's thought has also strongly influenced democratic education, both directly through the idea that the task of democratic education lies in the creation of the rational autonomous person, and indirectly through the idea that education is about the production of rational subjectivity.

Although the Kantian understanding of subjectivity has been very influential, it has also been fiercely criticized, both for its individualism and for its rationalism. Thinkers such as Nietzsche, Freud, and Foucault have all in their own way argued that the origin of subjectivity is not to be found in the subject's own rational thinking, but that subjectivity is constituted by forces and processes that are beyond rational control. Habermas has also criticized the individualistic rationalism of Kant, arguing that rationality is not the offspring of individual consciousness but emerges from the life of communication. In a similar vein, pragmatists like George Herbert Mead and John Dewey have questioned the Kantian framework, for both its individualism and its rationalism. For my discussion, Dewey is the most significant thinker, since his critique of and alternative for Kant's conception of subjectivity is closely connected to questions about education and democracy.

John Dewey: A Social Conception of the Democratic Person

Dewey's conception of subjectivity is, in a sense, as far away from the Kantian approach as possible. Whereas for Kant everything begins with the thinking activity of the rational being—Kant literally writes that the "I think" (*Ich denke*) is the "highest point to which we must ascribe all employment of the understanding" (Kant 1929, B134)—Dewey holds that mind is not "an original datum" but that it represents "something acquired" (Dewey 1980, 60). It is "an offspring of the life of association, intercourse, transmission, and accumulation rather than a ready-made antecedent cause of these things" (Dewey 1980, 60–61). This is Dewey's self-confessed Copernican Revolution, in which "the old center was mind" and the "new center is indefinite interactions" (Dewey 1984, 232). Against the "false psychology of original individual consciousness" (Dewey 1983, 62), Dewey presents human beings as *"acculturated* organisms" (Dewey 1988, 15), that is living organisms who, through their interaction with a social medium, form their habits, including the habits of thought and reflection.

The interaction with a social medium is not a one-way process in which newcomers simply take in the existing meanings and patterns of action of the group or culture they are part of. Interaction is participation, and participation is central to Dewey's understanding of communication. For Dewey communication is not the transfer of meaning from a sender to a receiver. It is a process of making something in common "in at least two different centers of behavior" (Dewey 1958, 178); it is "the establishment of cooperation in an activity in which there are partners, and in which the activity of each is modified and regulated by partnership" (Dewey 1958, 179). Communication, therefore, is a thoroughly *practical* process (Biesta 1994) in which patterns of action are formed and transformed, in which meanings are shared, recreated, and reconstructed, and through which individuals grow, change, and transform.

Dewey, of course, does not want to deny that human beings have the capacity for thought and reflection and that in this respect they are rational beings. What he does want to challenge is the whole philosophical tradition in which it is assumed that this capacity is an innate endowment. "Intelligence and meaning," as he writes in *Experience and Nature* "are natural consequences of the peculiar form which interaction sometimes assumes in the case of human beings" (Dewey

1958, 180). The "actuality of mind," as he writes elsewhere, "is dependent upon the education which social conditions set" (Dewey 1954, 209). The ability to think and reflect—which Dewey refers to as "intelligence"—can therefore be said to have a social origin, which is one way in which it can be argued that Dewey holds a social conception of subjectivity.

In a more general sense we can say that for Dewey we only become who we are through our participation in a social medium. This is what Dewey has in mind when he writes that education is a "social function, securing direction and development in the immature through their participation in the life of the group to which they belong" (Dewey 1966, 81). If this is so, then there are important educational questions to be asked about the "quality" of the life in which the *immature* (Dewey's term), or *newcomers* (my term), participate and learn. This is precisely the point Dewey makes in *Democracy and Education* when he argues that a social group in which there are many different interests and in which there is full and free interplay with "other forms of association" is to be preferred over a social group that is isolated from other groups and that is only held together by a limited number of interests. In the former kind of association there are many opportunities for individuals to develop and grow, whereas in the latter, these opportunities are limited and restricted. The education such a society gives, Dewey writes, is "partial and distorted" (Dewey 1966, 83). A group or society, on the other hand, in which many interests are shared and in which there is "free and full interplay with other forms of association" (Dewey 1966, 83) secures a "liberation of powers" (Dewey 1966, 87). The "widening of the area of shared concerns," and the "liberation of a greater diversity of personal capacities" are precisely what characterizes a "democratically constituted society" (Dewey 1966, 87).

It is important to see that Dewey is not simply saying that a more plural society provides more opportunities for individuals to choose from in developing their powers and capacities. Although this line of thinking is part of Dewey's social conception of subjectivity, Dewey does not conceive of the relationship between society and individuals as a one-way process in which individuals are shaped by society. For Dewey, the point is *not* the mere existence of different interests. What is crucial is the extent to which different interests are *consciously shared,* that is, the extent to which individuals are aware of the fact that their actions are part of the wider "social fabric" so that each individual "has to refer his own action to that of others, and to consider the action of others to give point and direction to his own" (Dewey 1966, 87). This adds a further dimension to Dewey's social conception of subjectivity, in that he argues that to be a subject or, as he sometimes calls it, an "individualized self" (Dewey 1954, 150), also means to take part in shaping the contexts that in turn shape individuality (see Festenstein 1997, 70). The idea of the subject as a shaper of the conditions that shape one's subjectivity is central to Dewey's understanding of the democratic person.

The kind of intelligence that is at stake in the shaping of the conditions that shape one's subjectivity is *social* intelligence. Social intelligence is both a requirement for and the outcome of participation in intelligent cooperation. As Carr and Hartnett explain: "By participating in this process, individuals develop those intellectual dispositions which allow them to reconstruct themselves and their social institutions in ways which are conducive to the realization of their freedom and to the reshaping of their society" (Carr and Hartnett 1996, 59). For Dewey this is what democracy is about, because in a democracy "all those who are affected by social institutions ... have a share in producing and managing them. The two facts that each one is influenced in what he does and enjoys and in what he becomes by the institutions under which he lives, and that therefore he shall have, in a democracy, a voice in shaping them, are the passive and active side of the same fact" (Dewey 1987b, 218).

For Dewey there is an intimate connection between democracy and education. This is first of all because he holds that democracy is that form of social interaction that best facilitates and supports "the liberation of human capacities for their full development" (Festenstein 1997, 72). Second, it is because we become a democratic person, that is, a person with social intelligence, through our participation in democratic life—which shows how Dewey's point of view exemplifies the idea of education *through* democracy. Along both lines we can see how Dewey's conception of the democratic person overcomes the individualism of the Kantian approach. In his views about democratic *education*, however, Dewey does remain caught in an instrumentalistic approach, in that he sees participation in democracy as the way in which the socially intelligent person is created or produced. In this respect we could even say that there is a trace of individualism in his views about democratic education, since for Dewey the democratic person is an individual with certain "attributes" or "qualities" (e.g., social intelligence), and the purpose of democratic education is to engender this individual. It is precisely at this point that Hannah Arendt's work allows us to develop a different understanding of democratic subjectivity.

Hannah Arendt: A Political Conception of the Democratic Person

As I have discussed in Chapter 4, Hannah Arendt's conception of subjectivity is rooted in her understanding of the active life, the *vita activa*. The *vita activa* is the life of *praxis*, which Arendt wants to restore to its proper place from which it had been dispelled since the beginning of Western philosophy by the life of contemplation, the *vita contemplativa*. Arendt distinguishes three dimensions of the active life: labor, work, and action. *Labor* is the activity that corresponds to the biological process of the human body. *Work*, on the other hand, is the activity that corresponds to the "unnaturalness" of human existence; it has to do with production and creation and instrumentality. It is concerned with making and therefore "entirely determined by the categories of means and end" (Arendt 1997b, 143). *Action,* on the other hand, is the activity "that goes on directly between men [*sic*]," without "the intermediary of things or matter" (Arendt 1977b, 7).

For Arendt, as we have seen, to act first of all means to take initiative, to begin something new, to bring something new into the world. Arendt characterizes the human being as an "*initium,*" as a "begin*ning* and a begin*ner*" (Arendt 1977a, 170; emphasis added). Action as beginning corresponds to the fact of birth, because with each birth something uniquely new comes into the world (see Arendt 1977b, 178). But it is not only when human beings are born that something uniquely new comes into the world. Arendt emphasizes that we continuously bring new beginnings into the world through everything we do.

Along these lines we can say that for Arendt subjectivity has to do with action: To be a subject means to act, and action begins with bringing one's beginnings into the world. The point is, however, that in order to act, in order to *be* a subject, we need others who respond to our beginnings. If I would begin something, but no one would respond, nothing would follow from my initiative, and, as a result, my beginnings would not come into the world and I would not *be* a subject. *I* would not come into the world. When, on the other hand, I begin something and others do take up my beginnings, I *do* come into the world, and in precisely this moment I *am* a subject. The problem is, however, that others respond to my initiatives in ways that are not predictable, because we always act upon beings "who are capable of their own actions" (Arendt 1977b, 190). It is, however, precisely the "impossibility to remain unique masters of what [we] do" that is at the very same time the condition—and the *only* condition—under which our beginnings can come into the world (Arendt 1977b, 220).

We could of course try to control the ways in which others respond to our beginnings—and Arendt acknowledges that it is tempting to do so. But if we would do this, we would make other human beings instruments for achieving our own purposes, which means that we would deprive them of their opportunities to being, their opportunities to bring themselves into the world through their own initiatives. We would deprive them of their opportunities to act and hence of their opportunities to *be* a subject.

This means that action, as distinguished from production (work), is never possible in isolation. This is why Arendt argues that "to be isolated is to be deprived of the capacity to act" (Arendt 1977b, 188). We need others, others who respond to our initiatives, who take up our beginnings, in order to be able to act and hence to be a subject. This also means, as we have seen, that action is never possible without plurality. As soon as we erase plurality, as soon as we erase the otherness of others by attempting to control how they respond to our initiatives, we not only deprive others of their actions, but at the same time, we deprive ourselves of our possibility to act, to come into the world, and to be a subject. In Arendt's terms we would have left the sphere of action and would have entered the domain of work.

Along these lines Arendt provides us with an understanding of human subjectivity in which subjectivity is no longer seen as an attribute of individuals, but is understood as *a quality of human interaction.* Arendt argues that subjectivity only exists *in action*—"neither before nor after" (Arendt 1977a, 153). This is, as we have seen, why she suggests that we should compare action and subjectivity with the performing arts. The main reason for this is that performing artists need an audience to show their "virtuosity" (Arendt), "just as acting men [*sic*] need the presence of others before whom they can appear" (Arendt 1977a, 154). The difference between performing arts and creative arts is, of course, not that creative arts—the arts of "making"—can do without an audience. The crucial point is that the work of art of the performing artist only exists *in* the performance—not before, not after. The script for a play may have endurance just as a painting; but it is only in the performance of the play that the play as a work of art exists. Similarly, individuals might have democratic knowledge, skills and dispositions, but it is only in action—which means action that is taken up by others in unpredictable and uncontrollable ways—that the individual can *be* a democratic subject.

Although we could refer to Arendt's ideas as a social conception of subjectivity—Arendt argues, after all, that we cannot be a subject in isolation—I prefer to call it a *political* conception. The main reason for this is that Arendt holds that *my* subjectivity is only possible in the situation in which others can be subjects as well. Not any social situation will therefore do. In those situations in which we try to control the responses of others or deprive others of the opportunity to begin, we cannot come into the world; subjectivity is not a possibility. Arendt relates subjectivity, in other words, to the life of the *polis,* the public sphere where we live—and *have* to live—with others who are not like us. It is precisely here that we can see the link with democracy, in that democracy can precisely be understood as the situation in which everyone has the opportunity to *be* a subject, that is, to act and, through their actions, bring their beginnings into the world of plurality and difference (see Biesta 2003b).

Education and the Democratic Person

Kant's conception of the democratic subject is clearly individualistic. He locates subjectivity in the individual's capacity for rational thinking. This is, of course, not unimportant, because to be a subject in a democratic society definitely involves the ability for critical and independent judgment. Although education plays an important role in Kant's approach, it is only to bring about rational powers that are already assumed to be there in some form or other. Education is supposed to support a process of the rational development of the individual. Moreover, Kant assumes that the rational powers of all individuals are basically the same. Rationality is not historically or socially contingent but ultimately universal. All individuals can, in principle, reach the state of enlightenment, the situation in which they can think for themselves. As long as they have not reached this stage, their development is not yet complete. Kant's conception of subjectivity is therefore also individualistic in its educational implications, because the task he sets for education is one that is aimed at the isolated individual. Kant provides, in other words, a rationale for a form of democratic education that focuses on the development of the individual's knowledge, skills, and dispositions—which is characteristic of what I have referred to as "education *for* democracy." The question Kant does not raise is the one about the social, material, and political *conditions* for subjectivity.

Dewey's social conception of the democratic person clearly brings these contextual dimensions into view. He acknowledges that we only become who we are through participation in a social medium and that to be a democratic subject or an "individualized self" means that we participate in the conditions that shape our individuality. Moreover, Dewey acknowledges that the intelligence we need for participation in social life is not a natural endowment, but is the outcome of our very participation in social interaction. We acquire *social* intelligence through our participation in democratic forms of cooperation. This places education in a different relationship to democracy, because with Dewey we can argue that education needs to provide opportunities for the formation of social intelligence, which means that education itself must be democratically organized. Dewey's conception of the democratic person thus provides a rationale for a form of democratic education that focuses on participation in democratic life as the way in which the democratic person is created—an approach characteristic of what I have called "education *through* democracy." In his views about democratic education, however, Dewey remains bound to an instrumentalistic and individualistic view, in that he sees participation in democratic life as the way in which the democratic person is created or engendered and also in that he sees the democratic subject as an individual with particular attributes or qualities, most notably the quality of "social intelligence."

Arendt's political conception of the democratic person introduces a different way of understanding human subjectivity. For Arendt subjectivity is not defined by the attributes of an individual but is understood as a quality of human interaction. Arendt radically situates our subjectivity *in* action—neither before, nor after. We *are* a subject in those situations in which our initiatives are taken up by others in such a way that the opportunities for others to bring their initiatives into the world are not obstructed. This line of thinking, as I will suggest in the next section, provides a rationale for an approach to democratic education that is distinctively different from the views that follows from a Kantian or Deweyan conception of democratic subjectivity.

Three Questions for Democratic Education

By locating subjectivity in the sphere of human interaction instead of "inside" the individual, Arendt allows us to think differently about the relationship between education and democracy. Her political conception of democratic subjectivity suggests a new set of questions for democratic education. Whereas traditional educational strategies focus on the question how to *prepare* children and newcomers for their future participation in democracy, Arendt urges us to get away from understanding education as the domain of preparation for something that will come later. Following Arendt we can say that education should not be seen as a space of preparation, but should be conceived as a space where individuals can act, where they can bring their beginnings into the world, and hence can be a subject. The educational question is therefore no longer that of how to engender or "produce" democratic individuals. The key educational question is how individuals can *be* subjects, keeping in mind that we cannot continuously be a subject, since we can only be a subject *in* action, that is, in our being *with others.*

From the point of view of democratic education this means that the first question to ask about schools and other educational institutions is not how they can make students into democratic citizens. The question to ask rather is: *What kind of schools do we need so that children and students can act?* Or, to put it in a way that can be used to examine actual educational practices: *How much action is actually possible in our schools?*

We might read this as Dewey's question about the democratic quality of educational institutions. Yet for Dewey and others who argue that the best education *for* democracy is education *through* democracy, the overarching aim is still to engender or "produce" democratic individuals. For me the issue is not how we can make schools (more) democratic *so that* children and students will become democratic persons. For me the question is whether democratic subjectivity is actually possible in schools. The question is, in other words, whether children and students can actually *be* democratic persons in the school. What we need to ask, therefore, is whether schools can be places where children and students can act—that is, where they can bring their beginnings into a world of plurality and difference in such a way that their beginnings do not obstruct the opportunities for others to bring their beginnings into this world as well.

What would this ask from schools? On the one hand it requires an educational environment in which students have a real opportunity to begin, to take initiative. It requires an educational environment that is not exclusively focused on the reproduction of the subject matter of the curriculum, but one that allows students to respond in their own, unique ways to the learning opportunities provided by the curriculum. This also requires a different understanding of the curriculum itself, one in which the curriculum is not simply seen as a set of knowledge and skills that needs to be transmitted to the students, but where different curricular areas are explored and used for the particular opportunities they provide for students to bring their own unique beginnings into the world. It requires, for example, that we do not approach language as a set of skills that students simply must acquire, but that we see it is as a human practice in which students can participate and through which they can find new ways of expressing themselves, new ways of bringing themselves into the world (see Biesta 2005). It further requires educators who show a real interest in the initiatives and beginnings of their students. And it requires an educational system that is not obsessed with outcomes and league tables, but that allows teachers to spend time and effort on finding the delicate balance between the child and the curriculum so that there are indeed real chances for children and students to undertake something new, "something unforeseen by us" (Arendt 1977a, 186).

We should not forget, however, that action is not only about beginning; it is also about the ways in which these beginnings are taken up by others who, as Arendt reminds us, are not only capable of their own actions but who should have the opportunity to act themselves as well. To act, that is to be a democratic person in a world of plurality and difference, is therefore as much about doing and saying and bringing oneself into the world, as it is about listening and waiting, creating spaces for others to begin, and thus creating opportunities for others to be a subject. This means that a democratic school, a school in which action is possible, is *not* a child-centered school, if, that is, we understand child-centeredness as self-expression without concern for others. Action is anything but self-expression; it is about the insertion of one's beginnings into the complex social fabric and about the subjection of one's beginnings to the beginnings of others who are not like us. The Arendtian conception of the democratic person thus calls for an approach to democratic education that is not child-centered but *action-centered*, one that focuses *both* on the opportunities for students to begin and on plurality as the only condition under which action is possible. It thus entails a double educational responsibility: a responsibility for each individual and a responsibility for "the world," the space of plurality and difference as the condition for democratic subjectivity.

Although these suggestions might seem rather general and abstract, they do hint at some of the key conditions under which action might be a possibility in schools. In this respect they do translate into concrete suggestions about how to make schools into places where action might happen and where individuals can be subjects, just as they indicate what might obstruct such opportunities. Schools that show no interest in what students think and feel, where there is no place for students to take initiatives, where the curriculum is only seen as subject matter that needs to be put into the minds and bodies of the students, and where the question about the impact of one's beginnings on the opportunities for others to begin is never raised, are clearly places where it is extremely difficult to act and to *be* a democratic subject. Yet such schools do exist, and young people are surprisingly well aware of the limitations this puts on their ability and the ability of others to come into the world and be a subject. It is in the routines of everyday life that the experience of democracy is "lived" and becomes real. The Arendtian conception of the democratic person therefore does not ask for a curriculum that produces the democratic individual, but instead asks for schools in which democracy—understood as action-in-plurality—is a real possibility. Such schools are not necessarily schools that are "democratic" in the more formal sense, for example, schools with a student parliament or schools based on the idea of democratic deliberation. Deliberation is, after all, only one of the ways in which individuals can act, can be a subject, and can come into the world—and it is not necessarily the way that fits everyone. There is, therefore, no blueprint of what a democratic school might look like, and there is no guarantee that what works at one point in time in one situation will also make action possible in other times and places. The question of how much action is possible in schools needs to be asked again and again and requires our constant attention.

If we give up the idea that education can produce the democratic individual and see democratic subjectivity as something that has to be achieved again and again, the question of action and democratic subjectivity is no longer one that is only relevant for schools: It extends to society at large and becomes a lifelong process. From the point of view of democratic education we should therefore not just ask how much action is possible in schools. We should also ask: *What kind of society do we need so that people can act?* Again, this question can also be phrased as a question for investigation into the democratic condition of a society: *How much action is actually possible in society?*

Both Dewey and Arendt can help us see that there is no point in blaming individuals for so-called antisocial or nondemocratic behavior, because individuals are always individuals-in-context. What Arendt can help us see, is that we also shouldn't expect that the problem can be solved by giving individuals a "proper" democratic education. Individuals do matter, but in a society or social setting in which individuals are not allowed to act—or in which only certain groups are allowed to act—we cannot expect that everyone will still behave in a "proper," democratic manner. What the Arendtian conception of the democratic person brings into view, therefore, is that we cannot simply blame education for the failure of democracy. The only way to improve the democratic quality of society is by making society more democratic, that is, by providing more opportunities for action—which is always action in a world of plurality and difference.

It may seem that the Arendtian emphasis on action implies that there is nothing left for educators to do. I do not think that this conclusion is correct. What my explorations do suggest, however, is a different way to understand the relationship between learning, subjectivity, and democracy. As I have shown, traditional approaches to democratic education ask how individuals can learn to *become* a democratic person. If democratic subjectivity only exists *in* action, if it is about coming into the world through the ways in which others respond to and take up our new beginnings, then the question of learning is not about how to become a subject, but *about learning from being and having been a subject.* The third question for democratic education suggested by the Arendtian point of view is, therefore, *What can be learned from being/having been a subject?*

The learning at stake here is learning from and learning about what it means to act, to come into the world, to confront otherness and difference in relation to one's own beginnings. To understand what it means to be a subject also involves learning from those situations in which one has *not* been able to come into the world, in which one has experienced for oneself what it means *not* to be able to act. Such an experience of frustration could, after all, be far more significant and have a much deeper impact than the experience of successful action. The role of schools and educators is therefore not just that of creating opportunities for action—both by allowing individuals to begin and take initiative and by keeping in existence a space of plurality and difference in which action is only possible. Schools and educators also have an important role to play in inviting and supporting reflection on those situations in which action was possible and, perhaps even more importantly, those situations in which action was *not* possible. This might foster an understanding of the fragile personal, interpersonal, and structural conditions under which human beings can act and can *be* a subject. It might foster an understanding of the fragile conditions under which everyone can be a subject and hence democracy can become a reality.

By asking these three questions—How much action is possible in our schools? How much action is possible in our society? What can be learned from being/having been a subject?—I propose to shift our thinking about democratic education away from an approach that puts the burden on individuals to behave democratically and on schools to create democratic individuals toward an approach that conceives of democracy as a situation in which all individuals can be subjects, in which they can all act in the Arendtian sense, in which they can all "come into the world." This, as I have tried to argue, does not mean that we all can simply do what we want. The crucial insight Arendt provides—an insight that is of immense importance for the "world of difference" (Säfström and Biesta 2001) we live in today—is that we can only be a subject in a world we share with others who are not like us and who are capable of their own actions. To be a subject, to "come into the world," is only possible if our beginnings are taken up by others in unprecedented, unpredictable, and uncontrollable ways. In this sense being a subject has indeed a dimension of being subjected to what is unpredictable, different, and other. Yet this is the paradoxical condition under which subjectivity can appear and under which democracy can become possible.

Conclusion

Ever since the Enlightenment there has been a strong tendency in educational theory and educational practice to think of education as the production of a subject with particular qualities, most notably the quality of rationality. This way of thinking has deeply influenced the theory and practice of democratic education and has led, as I have shown in this chapter, to an approach that is both instrumentalistic and individualistic. In this chapter I have shown that the way in which we understand and practice democratic education has everything to do with our conception of the democratic person. I have presented three different answers to the question as to what it means to be a democratic person: an individualistic, a social, and a political conception of democratic subjectivity. I have shown that each provides a different rationale for democratic education. Although the individualistic and the social conceptions are closely connected to ideas about democratic education as the production of the democratic individual (either by educational strategies directed at this individual, or by creating opportunities for individuals to participate in democratic life), I have shown that there is a different way to articulate what it means to be a democratic subject, and I have shown that this different, political conception of democratic subjectivity suggests a different set of questions for democratic education and hints at different educational practices.

Such an approach no longer focuses on the production of democratic individuals and no longer thinks of itself as having to prepare individuals for future democratic action. What schools can do—or at least should try to do—is to make action possible and hence create conditions for children and students to *be* subjects, to experience what it is and means to be a subject. The learning related to this is not something that comes *before* democratic subjectivity; it is not a kind of learning that produces democratic citizens. The learning that is at stake is a learning that follows from having been or, as I have also suggested, from having *not* been a subject. It is a learning about the fragile conditions under which action and subjectivity are possible—my subjectivity as much as the subjectivity of all others. Because subjectivity is no longer something that only occurs or is created in schools, the approach to democratic education that follows from my considerations puts the question about the responsibility for democratic education back where it actually belongs, namely, in society at large. It is an illusion to think that schools alone can produce democratic citizens. Insofar as action and subjectivity are possible in schools *and* society, schools can perform the more modest and more realistic task of helping children and students learn about and reflect upon the fragile conditions under which all people can act, under which all people can be a subject. A society in which individuals are not able or not allowed to act cannot expect its schools to produce its democratic citizens. The ultimate task for democratic education therefore lies in society itself, and *not* in its educational institutions. Schools can neither create nor save democracy—they can only support societies in which action and subjectivity are real possibilities.

A Pedagogy of Interruption

Education is the point at which we decide whether we love the world enough to assume responsibility for it and by the same token to save it from that ruin which, except for renewal, except for the coming of the new and young, would be inevitable. And education, too, is where we decide whether we love our children enough not to expel them from our world and leave them to their own devices, nor to strike from their hands their chances of undertaking something new, something unforeseen by us.

—Hannah Arendt

It seems appropriate to conclude this book with this quote from Hannah Arendt, because it captures in such a succinct manner, some of the central ideas that I have put forward in this book. Arendt speaks of a responsibility for the world— and of a love for the world underlying this responsibility; she speaks of the coming of the new and the young; and she summons us neither to leave the new and the young to their own devices, nor to block the opportunities for them to bring something new into the world, something that, because of its newness, cannot be foreseen by us. Arendt's words thus echo my point that the educational responsibility for the coming into presence of unique, singular beings entails a responsibility for the world—or, to be more precise, a responsibility for the *worldliness* of the world. She also makes it clear that educational responsibility requires a fine—or as I have put it, deconstructive—balance between engagement and openness. To focus on the coming into the world of new beginnings and new beginners does not mean that educators should simply stand aside and let things happen—which is why the language of learning is *not* the language of education. At the very same time, however, their engagement should not be one that tries to produce a particular kind of subjectivity, one that tries to bring about a particular kind of human being according to a particular definition of what it means to be human. The responsibility of the educator is a responsibility for what is to come, without knowledge of what is to come.

I have described the coming into presence of unique, singular beings itself in terms of responsibility. I have argued that what "makes" us unique, what "allows" us to speak in our own, singular voice, lies in the ways in which we respond to the other, to the otherness of the other. This is not, as Levinas reminds us, a question of *taking up* a responsibility, because that would assume that we are subjects, autonomous, sovereign subjects, before we become responsible. Responsibility is not "a simple attribute of subjectivity, as if the latter already existed in itself, before the ethical relationship" (Levinas 1985, 96). As Lingis explains, "(s)ubjectivity is opened from the outside by the contact with alterity" (Lingis 1981, xxi). Subjectivity-as-responsibility is therefore not a different way of being, because "being otherwise is still being" (Levinas 1985, 100). To understand the uniqueness of the human subject we must go "beyond essence," to a place—or better a nonplace, a "null-site" (Levinas 1981, 8) that is *otherwise than being* (Levinas 1981). The first question here is not that of the being of the subject but of "my right to be" (Levinas 1989b, 86). It is, therefore, in the "very crisis of the being of a being" (Levinas 1989b, 85), in the *interruption* of its being, that the uniqueness of the subject first acquires meaning. What constitutes me as this unique individual, as this singular being, is the point in time (which according to Levinas is actually the very beginning of temporality) at which I no longer deny the undeniable responsibility that is waiting for me. It is the point in time at which I respond to the other, keeping in mind that this response is always already a response to a "question" and not an act of recognition that would only bring the other into existence. The other exists before me. The uniqueness of the human being is thus to be understood in terms that go precisely against what Levinas calls the "ontological condition" of human beings. This is why he writes that to be human means "to live as if one were not a being among beings" (Levinas 1985, 100). What makes me unique is the fact that my responsibility is not transferable. "Responsibility is what is incumbent on me exclusively, and what, humanly, I cannot refuse. This charge is a supreme dignity of the unique. I am I in the sole measure that I am responsible, a non-interchangeable I. I can substitute myself for everyone, but no one can substitute himself for me" (Levinas 1985, 101)

This is why the educational concern for the uniqueness and singularity of the human being entails a concern and responsibility for the worldliness of the world, a concern for the creation of worldly spaces, spaces of plurality and difference. The encounter with otherness and difference is, after all, the difficult condition for the coming into the world of unique, singular beings. It is important to see that this is a necessary but never a sufficient condition. Even if we were able to create worldly spaces—and I have clearly indicated the limits of what can be created—there is no guarantee that individuals will respond to the otherness and difference they encounter and that they will do so in their own, unique ways. What can be known for sure, however, is that when spaces lose their worldly quality they cease to be spaces where action is possible and freedom can appear.

The educational responsibility is, however, not confined to the creation of and responsibility for worldly spaces. I have argued that there is also a more direct manifestation of educational responsibility that, following Levinas, we now might understand as an *interruption* of the being of a being, something that, in Chapter 1, I have referred to as the *violation* of the sovereignty of the subject. It entails asking the simple but in my view fundamental educational question: "What do you think about it?" (see Rancière 1991, 36; Masschelein 1998, 144; Biesta 1998a). This is a difficult question, a question with the potential to interrupt. Yet I wish to argue that it is also a question with the potential to call someone into being as a unique, singular individual. It is important to see that this question can be asked in many different forms. It is not necessarily about thinking. We can also ask, "Where do you stand on this?" or "How will you respond?" It can also be asked in nonverbal ways, for example by approaching the curriculum not as a set of knowledge and skills that has to be transferred into the minds and bodies of our students, but as a collection of practices and traditions that ask students for a response and that provide different ways for newcomers to respond and come into the world. In all cases, it means that education ceases to be a process of giving, and instead becomes a process of asking, a process of asking difficult questions.

In this book I have tried to give an answer to the question of what might follow if we give up the humanist foundations of education and, more specifically, the humanist foundations of modern education. My motivation for this exploration not only came from the insight that the attempt to define the essence and nature of the human being is impossible; in a sense such attempts always come too late, because in order to define the essence of the human being one has to *be* a human being first. It was also motivated by the claim that humanism is undesirable because it is not *sufficiently* human

(Levinas). This is why I have explored a way to understand and approach education in which the question of what it means to be human is seen as a radically *open* question, a question that can only be answered—and has to be answered again and again—by engaging *in* education, rather than as a question that needs to be answered *before* we can engage in education. I am aware that in taking this position I stand on the side of those who think that it is more dangerous to define what it means to be human than to leave this question open, and to leave it open in a radical way. To leave the question open is, of course, not without dangers either. I do believe, however, that to see the question of the humanity of the human being as a radically open question, as something that has to be "achieved" again and again, can help us to stay alert, particularly in the face of attempts to restrict what it means to be human and to lead a human life. This is, of course, more difficult than to live in a world in which it is clear who is human and who is not, a world in which it is clear who is rational and who is mad, who is civilized and who is not. But the sense of security that comes with such an approach can only ever be pseudosecurity, because the real question, how to live with others who are not like us, will not go away. This is why the critique of humanism and the alternative way to understand and approach education that I have developed in this book are intimately connected with the impetus, or, as some might say, with the promise of democracy. Democracy itself is, after all, a commitment to a world of plurality and difference, a commitment to a world where freedom can appear.

Bibliography

Apple, M. W. 1979. *Ideology and Curriculum*. Boston: Routledge and Kegan Paul.

———. 2000. "Can Critical Pedagogy Interrupt Rightist Policies?" *Educational Theory* 50 (2): 229–254.

Apple, M. W., and J. A. Beane. 1995. *Democratic Schools*. Alexandria, VA: Association for Supervision and Curriculum Development.

Arendt, H. 1977a (1954). *Between Past and Future: Eight Exercises in Political Thought*. Harmondsworth: Penguin.

———. 1977b (1958). *The Human Condition*. Chicago: University of Chicago Press.

———. 1982. *Lectures on Kant's Political Philosophy*. Chicago: University of Chicago Press.

Bailey, C. 1984. *Beyond the Present and the Particular. A Theory of Liberal Education*. London: Routledge and Kegan Paul.

Barber, B. 1984. *Strong Democracy. Participatory Politics for a New Age*. Berkeley: University of California Press.

———. 1998. *A Place for Us: How to Make Society Civil and Democracy Strong*. New York: Hill and Wang.

Barnes, B. 1977. *Interests and the Growth of Knowledge*. London: Routledge and Kegan Paul.

Bauman, Z. 1992. *Intimations of Postmodernity*. New York: Routledge.

———. 1993. *Postmodern Ethics*. Oxford: Blackwell.

————. 1995. "Making and Unmaking of Strangers." Reprinted in P. Beilharz, ed. 1999. *The Bauman Reader,* 200–217. Oxford: Blackwell.

————. 1999. *In Search of Politics.* Stanford, CA: Stanford University Press.

Beetham, D., and K. Boyle. 1995. *Introducing Democracy. 80 Questions and Answers.* Cambridge: Polity Press.

Bergers, G. 2003. "Individuality and Community—More Space for Development." *Detail. Zeitschrift fur Architektur/Review of Architecture* 43 (3): 226–236.

Bernstein, B. 2000. *Pedagogy, Symbolic Control and Identity.* Lanham, MD: Rowman and Littlefield.

Bhabha, H. K. 1990. "The Third Space. An Interview with Homi Bhabha." In J. Rutherford, ed. *Identity. Community, Culture, Difference,* 207–221. London: Lawrence and Wishart.

Biesta, G. J. J. 1994. "Education as Practical Intersubjectivity. Towards a Critical-Pragmatic Understanding of Education." *Educational Theory* 44 (3): 299–317.

————. 1998a. "'Say You Want a Revolution...' Suggestions for the Impossible Future of Critical Pedagogy." *Educational Theory* 48 (4): 499–510.

————. 1998b. "Pedagogy without Humanism. Foucault and the Subject of Education." *Interchange* 29 (1): 1–16.

————. 2001. "How Difficult Should Education Be?" *Educational Theory* 51 (4): 385–400.

. 2002a. "*Bildung* and Modernity. The Future of *Bildung* in a World of Difference." *Studies in Philosophy and Education* 21 (4/5): 343–351.

————. 2002b. "How General Can *Bildung* Be? Reflections on the Future of a Modern Educational Ideal." *British Journal of Philosophy of Education* 36 (3): 377–390.

————. 2003a. "Learning from Levinas: A Response." *Studies in Philosophy and Education* 22 (1): 61–68.

————. 2003b. "Demokrati—ett problem för utbildning eller ett utbildningsproblem?" *Utbildning and Demokrati* 12 1: 59–80.

————. 2004a. "Education, Accountability and the Ethical Demand. Can the Democratic Potential of Accountability Be Regained?" *Educational Theory* 54 (3): 233–250.

————. 2004b. "'Mind the Gap!' Communication and the Educational Relation." In Charles Bingham and Alexander M.

Sidorkin, eds. *No Education without Relation*, 11–22. New York: Peter Lang.

———. 2005. *"George Herbert Mead und die Theorie der schulischen Bildung."* In D. Troehler and J. Oelkers, eds. *Pädagogik und Pragmatismus. Gesellschaftstheorie und die Entwicklung der Pädagogik*, 131–150. Zürich: Verlag Pestalozzianum.

Biesta, G. J. J. and R. S. Lawy. 2006. "From Teaching Citizenship to Learning Democracy: Overcoming Individualism in Research, Policy, and Practice." *Cambridge Journal of Education* 36 (1): 29–45.

Biesta, G. J. J., and G. J. J. M. Stams. 2001. "Critical Thinking and the Question of Critique. Some Lessons from Deconstruction." *Studies in Philosophy and Education* 20 (1): 57–74.

Bloor, D. 1976. *Knowledge and Social Imagery*. London: Routledge and Kegan Paul.

Cadava, E., P. Connor, and J.-L. Nancy, eds. 1991. *Who Comes after the Subject?* New York: Routledge.

Callan, E. 1997. *Creating Citizens. Political Education and Liberal Democracy*. Oxford, UK: Oxford University Press.

Caputo, J. D. 1997. *Deconstruction in a Nutshell. A Conversation with Jacques Derrida*. New York: Fordham University Press.

Carr, W., and A. Hartnett. 1996. *Education and the Struggle for Democracy. The Politics of Educational Ideas*. Buckingham: Open University Press.

Cleary, J., and P. Hogan. 2001. "The Reciprocal Character of Self-Education. Introductory Comments on Hans-Georg Gadamer's Address 'Education Is Self-Education.'" *Journal of Philosophy of Education* 35 (4): 519–528.

Counts, G. 1939. *Dare the School Build a New Social Order?* New York: John Day.

Critchley, S. 1999. *Ethics—Politics—Subjectivity. Essays on Derrida, Levinas and Contemporary French Thought*. London: Verso.

Derrida, J. 1978. "Violence and Metaphysics. An Essay on the Thought of Emmanuel Levinas." In J. Derrida, *Writing and Difference*, 79–153. Chicago: University of Chicago Press.

———. 1988. *Limited Inc.* Evanston, IL: Northwestern University Press.

———. 1992. *The Other Heading. Reflections on Today's Europe*. Translated by Pascale-Anne Brault and Michael B. Naas. Bloomington: Indiana University Press.

———. 1997. *Politics of Friendship*. London: Verso.

———. 1998. *Monolingualism of the Other; or, the Prosthesis of Origin.* Stanford, CA: Stanford University Press.

Dewey, J. 1954. *The Public and Its Problems.* Chicago: Swallow Press.

———. 1958. *Experience and Nature.* New York: Dover Publications.

———. 1966 (1916). *Democracy and Education.* New York: Free Press.

———. 1980 (1917). "The Need for Social Psychology." In J. A. Boydston, ed., *John Dewey. The Middle Works, 1899–1924. Volume 10,* 53–63. Carbondale: Southern Illinois University Press.

———. 1983 (1922). *John Dewey. The Middle Works, 1899–1924. Volume 14: Human Nature and Conduct,* J. A. Boydston, ed. Carbondale: Southern Illinois University Press.

———. 1984 (1929). *John Dewey. The Later Works, 1925–1953. Volume 4: The Quest for Certainty,* J. A. Boydston, ed. Carbondale: Southern Illinois University Press.

———. 1987a (1937). "The Challenge of Democracy to Education." In J. A. Boydston, ed. *John Dewey. The Later Works, 1925–1953. Volume 11: 1935–1937,* 181–190. Carbondale: Southern Illinois University Press.

———. 1987b (1937). "Democracy and Educational Administration." In J. A. Boydston, ed. *John Dewey. The Later Works, 1925–1953. Volume 11: 1935–1937,* 217–252f. Carbondale: Southern Illinois University Press.

———. 1988 (1939). "Experience, Knowledge and Value: A Rejoinder." In J. A. Boydston, ed. *John Dewey. The Later Works, 1925–1953. Volume 14: 1939–1941,* 3–90. Carbondale: Southern Illinois University Press.

DfEE. 1998. *The Learning Age. A Renaissance for a New Britain.* Sheffield: Department for Education and Employment.

———. 1999. *Learning to Succeed. A New Framework for Post-16 Learning.* Sheffield: Department for Education and Employment.

Disch, Lisa Jane. 1994. *Hannah Arendt and the Limits of Philosophy. With a New Preface.* Ithaca: Cornell University Press.

Donald, J. 1992. *Sentimental Education. Schooling, Popular Culture and the Regulation of Liberty.* London: Verso.

Dreyfus, H. L., and P. Rabinow. 1983. *Michel Foucault. Beyond Structuralism and Hermeneutics. Second Edition. With an Afterword by and an Interview with Michel Foucault.* Chicago: University of Chicago Press.

Dryzek, J. S. 2000. *Deliberative Democracy and Beyond.* Oxford: Oxford University Press.

Eisenman, P. 1976. "Post-functionalism." Oppositions 6: unpaginated. Reprinted in K. Nesbitt, ed., *Theorizing a New Agenda for Architecture,* 80–83. New York: Princeton Architectural Press.

Englund, T. 1994. "Communities, Markets and Traditional Values: Swedish Schooling in the 1990s." *Curriculum Studies* 2 (1): 5–29.

Feinberg, W. 2001. "Choice, Autonomy, Need-Definition and Educational Reform." *Studies in Philosophy of Education* 20 (5): 402–409.

Festenstein, M. 1997. *Pragmatism and Political Theory. From Dewey to Rorty.* Chicago: University of Chicago Press.

Field, J. 2000. *Lifelong Learning and the New Educational Order.* Stoke on Trent: Trentham Books.

Fosnot, C. T. 1996. *Constructivism.* New York: Teachers College Press.

Foucault, M. 1973. *The Order of Things. An Archaeology of the Human Sciences.* New York: Vintage/Random House.

———. 1983. "The Subject and Power." In H. Dreyfus and P. Rabinow, *Michel Foucault. Beyond Structuralism and Hermeneutics. Second Edition. With an Afterword by and an Interview with Michel Foucault,* 208–226. Chicago: University of Chicago Press.

———. 1984. "What Is Enlightenment?" In P. Rabinow, ed., *The Foucault Reader,* 32–50. New York: Pantheon.

———. 1985. *The Use of Pleasure.* New York: Pantheon.

———. 1986. *The Care of the Self.* New York: Pantheon.

———. 1991. "The Ethics of Care for the Self as a Practice of Freedom. An Interview with Michel Foucault." In J. Bernauer and D. Rasmussen, eds., *The Final Foucault,* 1–20. Cambridge: MIT Press.

———. 1995 (1977). *Discipline and Publish. The Birth of the Prison.* New York: Vintage.

Gadamer, H.-G. 2001. "Education Is Self-Education." *Journal of Philosophy of Education* 35 (4): 529–538.

Gallie, W. B. 1955. "Essentially Contested Concepts." *Proceedings of the Aristotelian Society* LVI, 167–198. London: Harrison and Sons.

Ghirardo, D. 1996. *Architecture after Modernism.* London: Thames and Hudson.

Giesecke, H. 1985. *Das Ende der Erziehung.* Stuttgart: Klett-Cotta.

Giroux, H. A. 1989. *Schooling for Democracy. Critical Pedagogy in the Modern Age.* London: Routledge.

Granel, G. 1991. "Who Comes after the Subject?" In E. Cadava, P. Connor, and J.-L. Nancy, eds. *Who Comes after the Subject?,* 148–156. New York: Routledge.

Gutmann, A. 1987. *Democratic Education.* Princeton, NJ: Princeton University Press.

———. 1993. "Democracy." In R. E. Goodin and Ph. Pettit, eds. *A Companion to Contemporary Political Philosophy,* 411–421. Oxford: Blackwell.

Habermas, J. 1996. *Between Facts and Norms. Contribution to a Discourse Theory of Law and Democracy.* Cambridge, MA: MIT Press.

Heartfield, J. 2002. *The "Death of the Subject" Explained.* Sheffield: Sheffield Hallam University Press.

Heidegger, M. 1993 (1947). "Letter on Humanism." In David Farrell Krel, ed. *Martin Heidegger: The Basic Writings,* 213–265. San Francisco: Harper.

Held, D. 1987. *Models of Democracy.* Cambridge: Polity Press.

———. 1995. *Democracy and the Global Order. From the Modern State to Cosmopolitan Governance.* Cambridge: Polity Press.

Hertzberger, H. 2000. *Space and the Architect. Lessons in Architecture 2.* Rotterdam: 010 Publishers.

Honig, B. 1993. *Political Theory and the Displacement of Politics.* Ithaca, NY: Cornell University Press.

Kant, I. 1929. *Critique of Pure Reason.* Translated by N. Kemp Smith. New York: St. Martin's Press.

———. 1982. "Über Pädagogik." In I. Kant, *Schiften zur Anthropologie, Geschichtsphilosophie, Politik und Pädagogik,* 695–761. Frankfurt am Main: Insel Verlag.

———. 1992 (1784). "An Answer to the Question "What Is Enlightenment?" In P. Waugh, ed. *Post-Modernism: A Reader,* 89–95. London: Edward Arnold.

Klafki, W. 1986. "Die Bedeutung des klassischen Bildungstheorien für ein zeitgemässes Konzept von allgemeiner Bildung." *Zeitschrift für Pädagogik* 32 (4): 455–476.

Kurgan, L. 1994. "You Are Here: Information Drift." *Assemblage* 25: 14–43.

Laclau, E. 1995. "Universalism, Particularism, and the Question of Identity." In J. Rajchman, ed. *The Identity in Question,* 93–108. New York: Routledge.

Lave, J., and E. Wenger. 1991. *Situated Learning. Legitimate Peripheral Participation.* Cambridge: Cambridge University Press.

Levinas, E. 1981. *Otherwise Than Being or Beyond Essence.* The Hague: Martinus Nijhoff.

———. 1985. *Ethics and Infinity.* Pittsburgh, PA: Duquesne University Press.

———. 1989a. "Substitution." In S. Hand, ed. *The Levinas Reader,* 88–125. Oxford: Basil Blackwell.

———. 1989b. "Ethics as First Philosophy." In S. Hand, ed. *The Levinas Reader,* 75–87. Oxford: Basil Blackwell.

———. 1990. *Difficult Freedom. Essays on Judaism.* Translated by Seán Hand. Baltimore, MD: Johns Hopkins University Press.

———. 1998a. "The *I* and totality." In E. Levinas, *Entre-nous: On Thinking-of-the-Other,* 13–38. New York: Columbia University Press.

———. 1998b. "Uniqueness." In E. Levinas, *Entre-nous: On Thinking-of-the-Other,* 189–196. New York: Columbia University Press.

Lingis, A. 1981. "Translator's Introduction." In E. Levinas, *Otherwise Than Being or Beyond Essence,* xi–xxxix. The Hague: Martinus Nijhoff.

———. 1994. *The Community of Those Who Have Nothing in Common.* Bloomington: Indiana University Press.

Ljunggren, C. 1999. "Questions of Identity and Education. Democracy between Past and Future." In C.-A. Säfström, ed. *Identity. Questioning the Logic of Identity in Educational Theory,* 47–60. Lund: Studentlitteratur.

Løvlie, L., K. P. Mortensen, and S.-E. Nordenbro, eds. 2003. *Educating Humanity: Bildung in Postmodernity.* Oxford: Blackwell.

Masschelein, J. 1998. "In Defence of Education as Problematisation." In D. Wildemeersch, M. Finger, and R. Jansen, eds. *Adult Education and Social Responsibility,* 133–149. Frankfurt am Main: Peter Lang.

McDonnell, L., P. M. Timpane, and R. Benjamin, eds. 2000. *Rediscovering the Democratic Purposes of Education.* Lawrence: University Press of Kansas.

McLaren, P. 1997. *Revolutionary Multiculturalism. Pedagogies of Dissent for the New Millenium.* Boulder, CO: Westview Press.

McLaughlin, T. H. 2000. "Citizenship Education in England: The Crick Report and Beyond." *Journal of Philosophy of Education* 34 (4): 541–570.

McNeil, L. A. 2002. "Private Asset or Public Good: Education and Democracy at the Crossroads." *American Educational Research Journal* 39 (2): 243–248.

Mollenhauer, K. 1964. *Erziehung und Emanzipation.* Weinheim: Juventa.

Mouffe, Ch., ed. 1992. *Dimensions of Radical Democracy.* London: Verso.

———. 1993. *The Return of the Political.* London: Verso.

Nancy, J.-L. 1991. "Introduction." In E. Cadava, P. Connor, and J.-L Nancy, eds. *Who Comes after the Subject?*, 1–8. New York: Routledge.

Neill, F. 2004. "Fame Academy." *The Times Magazine.* (14 August): 39–41.

OECD (Organization for Economic Cooperation and Development). 1996. *Lifelong Learning for All.* Paris: OECD.

Parker, W. C. 1995. *Educating the Democratic Mind.* New York: SUNY.

Passerin d'Entrèves, M. 1994. *The Political Philosophy of Hannah Arendt.* London: Routledge.

Pateman, C. 1970. *Participation and Democratic Theory.* Cambridge: Cambridge University Press.

Peperzak, A. 1991. "Presentation." In R. Bernasconi and S. Critchley, eds. *Re-Reading Levinas*, 51–66. Bloomington: Indiana University Press.

Rancière, J. 1991. *The Ignorant Schoolmaster. Five Lessons in Intellectual Emancipation.* Stanford: Stanford University Press.

Rawls, J. 1993. *Political Liberalism.* New York: Columbia University Press.

———. 1997. "The Idea of Public Reason Revisited." *University of Chicago Law Review* 94, 765–807.

Säfström, C.-A. 2003. "Teaching Otherwise." *Studies in Philosophy and Education* 22 (1): 19–29.

Säfström, C.-A., and G. J. J. Biesta. 2001. "Learning Democracy in a World of Difference." *School Field* 12 (5/6): 5–20.

Saltman, K. J. 2000. *Collateral Damage: Corporatizing Public Schools—A Threat to Democracy.* Lanham, MD: Rowman and Littlefield.

Shapiro, I. 2003. *The State of Democratic Theory.* Princeton, NJ: Princeton University Press.

Sidorkin, A. M., and Ch. Bingham, eds. 2004. *No Education without Relation.* New York: Peter Lang.

Simons, J. 1995. *Foucault and the Political*. New York: Routledge.

Soder, R., J. I. Goodlad, and T. J. McMannon, eds. 2001. *Developing Democratic Character in the Young*. San Francisco: Jossey-Bass.

Torney-Purta, J., R. Lehmann, H. Oswald, and W. Schulz. 2001. *Citizenship and Education in Twenty-Eight Countries: Civic Knowledge and Engagement at Age Fourteen*. Amsterdam: IEA.

Torres, C. A. 1998. *Democracy, Education and Multiculturalism. Dilemmas of Citizenship in a Global World*. Lanham, MD: Rowman and Littlefield.

Tschumi, B. 1981. *The Manhattan Transcripts*. New York: St. Martin's Press.

———. 1994a. "Urban Pleasures and the Moral Good." *Assemblage* 25: 6–13.

———. 1994b. *Architecture and Disjunction*. Cambridge, MA: MIT Press.

———. 1994c. *Event-Cities*. Cambridge, MA: MIT Press.

———. 2001. *Event-Cities 2*. Cambridge, MA: MIT Press.

Usher, R., and R. Edwards. 1994. *Postmodernism and Education*. London: Routledge.

Vanderstraeten, R., and G. J. J. Biesta. 2001. "How Is Education Possible?" *Educational Philosophy and Theory* 33 (1): 7–21.

Wells, A. S., J. Slayton, and J. Scott, J. 2002. "Defining Democracy in the Neoliberal Age: Charter School Reform and Educational Consumption." *American Educational Research Journal* 39 (2): 337–361.

Westheimer, J., and J. Kahne. 2004. "What Kind of Citizen? The Politics of Educating for Democracy." *American Educational Research Journal* 41 (2): 237–269.

Wimmer, K-M. 1988. *Der Andere und die Sprache*. Berlin: Reimer Verlag.

Index

Abortion, 79, 104

Accountability, 19, 25

Action, 85–87, 88, 133, 139; agent-revealing capacity of, 83; conditions for, 94–95; democracy and, 123, 135; democratic, 121, 141; described, 47; freedom and, 86, 92–93; frustration of, 82; in Greek/Roman political context, 84; human, 49, 107, 108; isolation and, 84; natality and, 48; passion and, 52; performance and, 87, 135; plurality and, 81, 89, 140; predicament of, 83–85; realm of, 93; schools and, 141; subjectivity and, 134, 141, 144, 145; work and, 82

Adult Education, 15

Alfred Lerner Hall, 109–111

Analytic of finitude, 38

Anthropoemic strategy, 59

Anthropological question, 40

Anthropophagic strategy, 58–59

Architect, responsibility of, 115

Architecture, 100; end of, 114; functionalism of, 109, 110; Modern Movement in, 108; Renaissance, 44; space of, 44–47; theory of, 45, 46

Arendt, Hannah, xii, 51, 121; on action, 47, 49, 81, 82, 84–85, 92–93, 133, 139; antisocial/nondemocratic behavior and, 141; on boundlessness, 85; deconstruction and, 92; democratic person and, 132–135, 137; on disclosure, 83; on freedom, 85–86, 87, 88, 92–93; on human beings, 48; on human interaction, 47, 76; on isolation, 134; on labor, 80; on performing arts, 86–87; pluralism/judgment and, 90; on plurality, 80, 82, 87, 92; politics and, 80–83, 85, 88, 126; on publicity, 90; on responsibility, 147–148; subjectivity and, 132, 133, 135, 137; as *virtù* theorist, 77; on visiting, 92

Assimilationism, 60, 91

Atrocities, humanism and, 6

Autonomy, education and, 4, 36

Bauman, Zygmunt: *anthropophagic* and, 58; modern society and, 57, 58, 59; postmodern society and, 60; on stranger, 59; on subjectivity, 61, 69–70; TINA and, 98

Beetham, on democracy, 122

Beginning, 84, 133–134

Being, 107; interruption of, 149; truth of, 40

Being-in-the-world-with-others, 50

Being-with-others, 51

Bentham's Panopticon, 109, 113

Bhabba, Homi, 102

Bildung: concept of, 2, 3, 12n1, 101; education and, 100–102; paradox of, 114–116; question of, 101; self-, 3, 101; tradition of, 11–12n1, 99–100, 102, 106; worldly space and, 105–108

Boundlessness, 84, 85

Boyle, on democracy, 122

Building, paradox of, 114–116

Buildings, use of, 108

Developmental psychology, educational theory/practice and, 35
Dewey, John: antisocial/nondemocratic behavior and, 141; communication and, 36; on democracy/education, 122, 131–132, 136, 138; democratic person and, 128–132, 136; on human beings, 129; on intelligence, 129, 130; language and, 13; social conception of, 126; subjectivity and, 131
Difference, 49, 76, 87, 94, 103; cultural, 102; democracy and, 151; diversity and, 102; otherness and, 149; plurality and, 92, 120; problems with, 79; space of, 11, 93, 100, 115, 140, 142, 149; worldly space and, 112; world of, 9, 10, 11, 54, 107, 117–118, 135, 139, 141, 143
Disch, Lisa, 87, 89, 90, 95n1
Discipline, 2, 101
Dissent, pluralism and, 78
Diversity, 76, 79, 87, 94; difference and, 102

Ecological problems, 15, 105
Economic transaction, education as, 19, 21, 24, 31
Educating Rita (Russell), 21
Educating the Democratic Mind (Parker), 123
Education: actuality of mind and, 130; becoming somebody and, 94; beginning of, 25; community of, 67–69; concept of, 15; deconstructive nature of, 11, 75; democracy and, 119, 125–126, 128, 131–132, 136; as deviation, 74; difficulty of, 74–76, 92–95; emancipatory language of, 14, 15; engaging in, 26; essentials of, 94; for, 31–32; improvement of, 74; institutionalized places of, 121; language of, 10, 13, 14, 118, 148; marketization of, 118; metaphor for, 93; modern, 3, 4, 9, 17, 31, 35–36, 150; possibility of, 75, 94; purpose of, 98–99; questions about, 28–29; responsibility for, 147; revisiting, 118–121; role of, 4, 21, 22, 58, 70, 97, 120, 130, 143; subject of, 34–37;

technological expectations about, 73–74; theory/practice of, 15, 19, 35; understanding, 20–21, 32, 99, 117. *See also* Democratic education
Educational process, 69, 74, 75, 116
Educational questions, 2, 23, 29, 31, 54, 137
Educational relationships, 15, 29, 30, 31; constitution of, 24, 26, 32
Educational response, 100, 102
Educators: providers and, 20; responsibility of, 9, 32, 115, 142, 148
Edwards, Richard, 34–35
Efficiency, model of, 110
Ego cogito, 37, 40, 50
Eisenman, Peter, 44, 45
Emancipation, 14, 60
Emergence of man, 38, 39
Empathy, 91, 92
End of man, 7, 8, 34, 37–41, 53
Enlightenment, 2, 4, 95n1, 100, 119, 127, 143; blocking progress in, 3; defined, 35, 101; heritage of, 17; motto of, 3
Epistemology, 70, 127
Ethics, 50–52, 53, 54, 65, 66, 103
European Commission, lifelong learning and, 16
Euthanasia, 79, 104
Event, space and, 46, 110
Exclusion, strategy of, 59
Experience and Nature (Dewey), 129

Feinberg, on market models, 21
Field, John, 18
Form-follows-function formula, 44–45
Forms of life, 36
Foucault, Michel, xii, 37, 53, 128; approach and, 41; on Classical Age, 38; emergence of man and, 38, 39; end of man and, 7, 34; humanism and, 40; language and, 13; subjectivity and, 39; work of, 39, 40
Frederic the Great, 101
Freedom, 85–87, 151; action and, 86, 92–93; appearance of, 87–89; as beginning, 85; inner, 85, 86; possibility of, 92; public character of, 86; question of, 85; as virtuosity, 88

About the Author

Gert J. J. Biesta is Professor of Educational Theory at the University of Exeter, England, and Editor-in-Chief of *Studies in Philosophy and Education*. He is coauthor of *Pragmatism and Educational Research* (with Nicholas Burbules, Rowman & Littlefield 2003) and coeditor of *Derrida and Education* (with Denise Egéa-Kuehne, Routledge 2001).